You Aren't Depression's Victim!

By Debra Atlas

You Aren't Depression's Victim!
Table of Contents

Introduction   **1**

Chapter 1   **4**
- When Humpty Dumpty Fell Apart – Preludes and Tsunamis

Chapter 2   **15**
- Crashing Waves: Disability and "ah ha" Moments

Chapter 3   **20**
- Being a Pet Mom and Seeing the Mirror

Chapter 4   **26**
- Deeper Dives, Lessons, Opportunities and Choices

Chapter 5   **33**
- Dancing Through an Ocean of Tears

Chapter 6   **41**
- Expectations and Rabbit Hole Revelations

Chapter 7   **46**
- Depression's Nuts, Bolts and Surprising Links

Chapter 8   **55**
- Being Tough Ain't What It's Cracked Up to Be: Mis-Perceptions Revealed and Depression's Gifts

Chapter 9   **62**
- Still Gotta Long Way to Go: Grief and Loss Take Center Stage

Chapter 10   **67**
- A Different View of Life: Choices Discovered

Chapter 11   **73**
- Living with Gratitude, Connecting & Being of Sevice

Chapter 12   **79**
- What Happens When ... Questions to Dive Into

Chapter 13   **83**
- Miracles, Challenges and Loss Equals More Choice

Chapter 14   **92**
- Different Directions Bring Surprises and Changing Your Conversation

Chapter 15   **101**
- Not an Ending - an Empowering Beginning

Reflections to Ponder   **108**

Acknowledgments   **110**

To my Mother, Rita Atlas.
You encouraged me to finish this book
when I wasn't sure I should - or could.
I'm forever grateful and I miss you very much.

Introduction

**"You are a rich and creative spiritual being.
You can never be less than this. You may
frustrate your potential.
You may identify with that which is less than
what you can be. But within you now and
always is the unborn possibility of
a limitless experience of inner stability and
outer treasure, and yours is the privilege of
giving birth to it.
And you will, if you believe.**

—Eric Butterworth, Spiritual Economics

This book encompasses many things – the aftermath of several car accidents, health crises and personal and spiritual lessons that were part of my "recovery." Most of all, it's about discovery – about strengths I didn't know I had, lessons learned that have guided me over time, and discovering I was a part of something.

People talk about "community." That's a concept I've had difficulty understanding, yet for years I've struggled to do so. Pairing this concept with ideas like "interconnectedness" and "service", this idea will be a running thread throughout this book.Like so many people, I've had my share of challenges – physical (health-related), financial, and emotional. Part of my challenge has been that I've always had a different perspective of life. I view life as a tapestry. And it's been difficult to see where threads began or to make sense of how they weave in and out. Yet as challenging as it's been, I believe this perspective has helped me develop my sense of faith – faith that things will work out how they're supposed to, and that when and if I'm supposed to understand then I will.

Worrying is tough on both the body and the spirit. I'm still working on accepting that worrying isn't helpful.I've learned a lot about letting go; it's an on-going life lesson. It's also an important key to staying balanced in life. Maintaining balance can be difficult to do, but I'm getting better at it. It's surprising how much easier life gets when you quit worrying, take whatever actions/steps you can, then let things go the way they're meant to go.

When I say balance and letting go, I don't mean "going with the flow." That's too passive an interpretation for me. I mean recognizing when it's time to take action – effective, organized, concentrated effort – and then, after doing all you can, letting things move forward organically. If you think that sounds easy, think again! It's taken me years to write this book. During that time, many things tested my spirit and my beliefs – including deep loss, long periods of depression, even a raging pandemic. But during all that time, I also had periods where I was "depression free" - times when I felt balanced, enabled, focused; when the shadow of depression had lifted. To my knowledge, nothing caused it to happen. It just did. The first time this happened, the feeling of freedom was remarkable. This lasted about a week. The second time around, which lasted a bit longer, I tried to grasp how it had happened and how to explain it. Needless to say, I am extremely grateful for these experiences. They not only freed me up, they enabled me to see patterns that help me stay more balanced in the face of despair. This in turn helps me in my present day life to not "go down the rabbit hole." Perhaps after reading this book you'll have some understanding of this for yourself.

Let me be very clear here. This book isn't meant to replace therapy or any medical resources you might be considering or are already taking advantage of. Having lived with depression for decades, I know the value of utilizing those resources and how crucial they are. Having them available has helped me live a fuller, more creative life. There are many ways to approach this book. One would be to use it as an added tool in your tool kit to help illuminate the bigger picture. This may help smooth the path along your journey. Some of the thoughts I've gleaned from this boulder-filled journey might be useful to you. They may help you understand more about yourself, how you think and what's possible for you.My advice? Use what fits, then let the rest go. So, happy reading. Take some notes along the way. You just might discover steps – or additional threads – to help you move forward and help you stop being depression's victim!

Chapter 1

When Humpty Dumpty Fell Apart – Preludes and Tsunamis

You gain strength, courage and confidence by every experience in which you really stop to look fear in the face.

… You must do the thing you think you cannot do.

--- Eleanor Roosevelt

Preludes

If there's one thing I've learned along my life's journey, it's that living with depression can be hard. You can get so far down, you don't realize that's what's happening. The lows can be as deep as the Grand Canyon, the highs euphoric. It can be a crazy continuing roller coaster ride.

Some people handle stress, disappointments, and tough circumstances well. With me, my emotions can take over. When I'm depressed, everything's amplified, which makes it difficult when I try to explain to someone what I'm going through.

I've lived with depression since at least age two. As a child, I felt shy, separate, deeply sad, different from the rest of my family and friends. I felt odd man out – at home, at school, almost everywhere. And being in crowds or large groups – even if they were people I knew – were difficult for me. I'd often cover up my shyness and discomfort. But during events such as when my parents entertained in our home, I'd often retreat to my bedroom or my bathroom for an hour or more, just to get away. That was the only way I could cope with my overwhelming shyness and sadness. Then I'd slip back into the party as if nothing had happened.

The peculiar thing was, my shyness wasn't ongoing. There were times I seemed fine and enjoyed being with groups.

But then wham – I'd suddenly be overwhelmed with painful shyness and would have to retreat. I never saw it coming. Its unmistakable appearance meant I suddenly couldn't handle being sociable.

These sudden attacks of shyness weren't limited to my growing up years. As an adult, I've suffered through a number of these. For no reason at all, a shyness attack would hit and I'd shrink away from everyone, particularly at a group event. It was so painful and yet I had no control over what was happening.

Some would call these panic attacks. For me , it wasn't about panic. Physically I felt fine. I didn't experience any shortness of breath, no sweating or heart palpitations. I just couldn't be a part of a group when this happened. The overwhelming feeling I had was that of being intensely shy and needing to be alone. Once that passed, I was able to rejoin the group.

An example was at my Father's 70th birthday party, an elegant black tie affair. Even though the several hundred or so attendees included many people I'd known for years, I found myself tongue-tied throughout the evening. When it came time to give toasts and testimonies to and about my Father, I couldn't. Everyone else in my family stood up and gave glowing toasts to my Dad. I begged off. I was too intensely stuck in the pain of my shyness to get up and say a word. Me – who'd had a career as a singer, performer and, yes, a professional speaker – I could not stand in front of friends and family to honor my father on this important occasion. It's one of the few regrets I carry still, yet at the time there was nothing I could do about it.

I never understood these feelings. But they left me feeling even more disconnected and isolated, often like I was letting people down. This added to my feeling of loneliness.

In my family, we pretty much aimed to be Type A's. Overachieving wasn't considered a bad thing. The underlying message we learned was that with focus, practice and hard work, you could achieve practically anything. But striving for perfection – that added edge that as an "average" kid I felt I could never reach, increased my feelings of inadequacy and disconnection, especially with my parents.

When I was growing up, my Dad traveled a lot for business. We never knew if he was in or out of town until we gathered around the dinner table. And my Mom? When she wasn't traveling with my Dad, she had the daunting task of tending to four active young kids.

When both my parents were away, one of a select group of ladies came to stay with us. I remember three of them, all of whom to my young eyes seemed elderly, although as I am approaching my seventh decade, I wonder if that was just my perspective. Mrs. Cummings, Mrs. Savage and Mrs. York were good substitutes for my folks, making sure we not only "towed the line" as it were but also took care of us if we got sick. And as I seemed to get many of my childhood diseases each time my parents went away, I was often their focus. My Mom would tell them that I would probably get sick while they were gone and not to worry. Apparently my sense of abandonment manifested into measles (twice), chicken pox and the flu. I guess my illnesses were the only way I could feel safe without my parents around.

My Mom and I were like fire and water when I was growing up. She would say black and I would say white. A classic example was when, as a youngster, we were at the swimming pool. Mom warned me not to go near the deep water but, next thing she knew, there I was, almost drowning. Fortunately, a lifeguard came to my rescue and saved me. I learned of this years later when my folks introduced me to him and told me the story.

There's a huge gap between being adventurous and being a happy kid.. I rarely remember being happy growing up. It wasn't part of my vocabulary. Sad, morose, moody – those were feelings I understood and was familiar with.

As a young child, I was clear I didn't measure up. In our family, being average wasn't something to aspire to. Excelling was. My older brother, who I adored, was popular, incredibly intelligent and well thought of. And as much as he excelled academically, I seemed to limp along. I wasn't a bad student, but I struggled. My brother's special skill and talent in Math was to me a foreign language I couldn't decipher. And for me, that was the same as failing.

One can never judge a book by its cover, or people either. Growing up, on the outside, I was a tomboy – active, always participating in neighborhood games and activities, seemingly a happy kid. But on the inside, I was bombarded with feelings of inadequacy, painful shyness, sadness and depression, although I didn't have those words for all that then. To me, it seemed that there was no where to turn and no way out.

My day-to-day family environment felt like a tangled web of angst, sadness and feeling separate. But there was a small silver lining – a temporary path to freedom. My bicycle – my semi-mechanical steed that would whisk me away from the upset of daily life. There was a secluded place near our house that I'd often ride my bike to. I could hide there, unobserved, surrounded by Nature. In the late 1950s and early 60s – in the small town in South Texas where I grew up, where no one locked their doors – a child alone, away from adults or anyone else, wasn't the problem it would be today.

My secret place was my haven, my place to be alone. There, surrounded by Nature's beauty and serenity, I'd release my pent-up anger and frustration at the crazy mess my life seemed to be. In this safe place, I was finally free – from feeling wrong, from feeling I didn't belong. I spent countless hours there, weeping, pleading to whoever / whatever might be listening for clarity, for understanding; emptying out my soul in the only way I knew how. And somehow, the relative quiet I found there brought me comfort. And although my weeping yielded no answers, I would eventually find a little calmness before riding back home to face life again.

But life moves forward and circumstances change. When I was thirteen, we moved to a new house and I lost that safe space. After sharing a room with one of my sisters for years, I suddenly had my own room and some privacy. But that meant more time to be alone, more time to grapple with family issues and my growing despair. I deeply felt the loss of my safe haven. Perhaps that loss contributed to what took place months later.

The Tsunamis

Earthquakes, while almost never predictable, can create life-shattering tsunamis. In our own lives, early warnings rarely happen before our own personal tsunamis hit.

Talking about these times in my life isn't easy. Before we get to the dark times of my own tsunamis, let me tell you about a bright, joyous time. As I said, happy was a rarity and joy even rarer. But as a young teenager, one bright time stands out.

Something magical happened at the end of my seventh grade school year, I tried out for the school choir. Now that may not seem big to you but to me, it was huge. I'd always sung – to myself, around the house, in the shower. But as a shy person who often felt inadequate, I'd never sung in front of anyone. When I read the notice for after-school choir tryouts, I thought: "maybe this is something I can do, something that could be all mine, something I could be good at." Grasping at an elusive brass ring, I took a chance – and I made it!

My family was surprised. Me, singing? Taking initiative and trying out for something new and different? That was totally out of character. Later I learned that my Dad had sung in the choir at our Temple when I was young. At this point, however, no other family member was involved in singing. That would come later when my sisters got to high school. For now, this was something special for me, something I excelled at.

That sense of achievement, of being able to shine, was new to me and I reveled in it. During the middle of my freshman year of high school, I was promoted to the senior choir – the only freshman at that point to have achieved that honor. That had me flying with pride and happiness! Finally I was being recognized for something, some achievement. I was a star in the family! I was finally out of my brother's shadow. And for a while, I knew joy.

But as I said earlier, my sense of happiness was fleeting.

After all, I was a teenager and, at its best, that is challenging. For me, the time leading up to and during my 14th year was one of the most painful of my life. That was when I tried to end things.

There wasn't a clear path that led me there, but there were steps along the way. Here are some of them.

Growing up, I had a rocky relationship with my family and silence was my safe mode. I was known as the "Stone Face". Offering my opinion, which invariably was different than everyone else's, or asking any thought-provoking questions, usually got me into trouble. So keeping my thoughts to myself was always a safer choice.

As a kid, I'd always been a night owl. The family usually was asleep by around 9pm and that's when I seemed to get my second wind. Many's the night I'd sneak into the family room when the house was quiet to watch old movies on TV. Invariably my Mother would find me and send me off to bed. I missed the last 10 to 15 minutes of lots of movies!

After moving into the new house, sleeping through the night became even more difficult. In 1966, less than a year after moving into our new house, I began experiencing terrible insomnia almost nightly. I'd toss and turn all night, finally falling asleep from exhaustion; waking in the morning to find the bedding thrown across the room.

Adding to this mix, even though ours was a newly built house, somehow mice had gotten stuck in the wall and migrated to the wall where my bed was. Many nights I'd hear them squeaking and clawing. Several nights I'd be jolted awake to discover they'd somehow fallen into the wastebasket beside my bed! Can you picture me bolting straight up out of an exhausted sleep and practically hitting the ceiling! That's right. Any wonder I didn't want to sleep at night?

After a few nights of "mousecapades", workers finally located the holes the mice had used to get into my room and sealed them up. But even so, my insomnia and dread of falling asleep persisted. Eventually our family doctor prescribed sleeping pills to hopefully help me get some much needed rest. I took them every night for months, praying for deep sleep that seldom came.

Mice tumbling into the wastebasket by the bed; rampant insomnia and plenty of sleeping pills at hand. A healthy prescription for a happy teenager, right? Not really. These factors contributed to my growing sense of life gone wrong during those first years in our new home. Undiagnosed depression played a big role in my life, but, back then, people didn't talk about depression. This was especially true in my family. But, for me, dark clouds were gathering during those years; ignorance, denial and a family crisis would nearly cost me my life.

During 1966-1067, my family hosted an exchange student in our home for a year. He was a quiet but fun-loving, independent soul. One day, he wandered off without telling anyone in the family where he'd gone. Hours later, when my parents discovered he was missing, havoc reigned. Where was he? Had something happened? Was he in trouble? What could we do to find him?

Remember, up until that time, I was the family's "stone face". But this was a family crisis.

Determined to help, I stepped out of my silence and took action. I boldly picked up the phone and called everyone I knew, trying to find him or at least see if anyone knew where he might be. I thought this was the best way to help. Today we'd call that networking. Then it was just reaching out to friends.

When I reported back to my folks what I'd done and that no one had seen or heard from him, it was as if a brick wall fell on my head. My family was well known throughout our community and my parents were FURIOUS! Apparently, they thought my actions had made them look bad.

Their reaction was:

- How could I tell everyone we knew we'd "lost" our exchange student?

- What would everyone think? Or, more accurately, how would they judge my family?

- And, more importantly, WHAT WAS I THINKING???

Ultimately, our exchange student returned, unaware of the havoc his adventure had created. But the interim, for me, was life altering, and almost tragic.

Being emotionally fragile, my family's reaction devastated me. Two things became crystal clear to me. The first: that my life was hopeless. And second, I realized that I couldn't make a difference no matter what I did. My life and everything about it looked bleak, black and impossible. My despair was complete and overwhelming. Seeing no hope and no other obvious options, I chose the only path forward I saw – to try and end it all as quickly as possible.

The idea of suicide wasn't something completely new to me. I'd thought about it before but I'd never told anyone. I'd kept things bottled up inside for years. Although I was often surrounded by friends and friends of the family – people I loved and respected – I never felt I had anyone I could share my all-encompassing deep pain with. For years, nothing in my life felt safe. So things just kept building and building – until that last shoe fell.

When it did, when I felt there was no hope; the excruciating pain I felt drove me to my bedroom – the only familiar semi-safe place I had. There, I opened the ever-present bottle of sleeping pills on the nightstand beside my bed and swallowed its contents – lots of shiny red gels. There was no thought of anything except despair and wanting to stop the excruciating pain and suffering I felt.

There are those who say that people who commit suicide are selfish; that they don't think about the impact their actions have on those who love them, how devastated those they leave behind will be. But to me, what's real and true is very different than that.

When I tried to kill myself by swallowing all those sleeping pills, I was trying to stop the excruciating pain. I was devastated, isolated, feeling worthless and saw no other way out. I can say from personal experience that NO THINKING takes place when someone acts to take their own life. Thinking about cause and effect takes a different ability that someone considering suicide simply doesn't have. There's no thought, no larger picture.

Nothing. As a teenager who'd lived with a silent yet escalating sense of hopelessness, when the last shoe fell, no hole was big enough to crawl into to save myself. Suicide – ending my pain and excruciating suffering – was the only path open to me.

But to finish the story.

Fortune smiled on me that evening. At that time, my family had two phone lines – one for the folks and one for us kids. Shortly after I took those pills, a good friend of mine called me on the kids phone line. Learning what I'd done, she hung up and called another friend who called me back and kept me talking while my other friend told her parents. They then called my folks and I was "saved."

The repercussions of trying to understand and deal with the aftermath of this situation left my parents upset and struggling to make some sense of it all. And it left me overwhelmed and confused. When you've sunk to the depths of despair and have given up on life, moving "up" seems an impossible task. Wanting to live, to come back fully into life, is incredibly difficult. And for parents whose child has reached that point when they had no clue about it, that must have devastated them to their core, made them question everything they thought they knew or believed.

But positive things can emerge from the negative. That night, in the hospital, with a tube threaded down my throat to pump my stomach, that was the first time I remember my folks telling me they loved me.

I'm sure they'd told me before. But truthfully, until this incident, I had no memory of them saying it. Would it have made a difference if they'd said it more often before this crisis happened? Perhaps. But that wasn't how the cards played out. My parents weren't demonstrative people, although they cared deeply about their family and friends. Butit took a crisis that could have ended my life for my parents to voice their love to me.

So what did I learn from this? As painful as these memories have been to relive, doing so has helped me realize how human my parents were.

I was the second child in my family – the one after the almost perfect son whom everyone adored, he who excelled at practically everything he tried. My parents had no idea what to do with a teenage child so distraught she would attempt to take her own life. Not being a family that talked things out, they did what they could. I cannot imagine the pain and anguish they must have felt.

They reached out to our family doctor and other "experts" to see where to turn, what to do. Ultimately, they took me to see a shrink in Houston, but without telling me about him or the reason for the visit. When we arrived at the office complex, because I'd already been to see another doctor in that same building, I was none the wiser. It was only when we stepped off the elevator at a different floor and went to a different doctor's office and I saw that the name on the door said "psychologist" that I realized something was different.

Walking in the door – my parents stayed outside while I walked in alone – I learned why I was there. Stunned, I sat down and once again retreated into silence. I felt completely betrayed, confused, upset. I didn't say a word the entire time I was there. This onetime visit was an absolute failure.

I'm sure my parents were worried, but, true to form, we never discussed it – ever. I was never sent to another psychiatrist or psychologist; life went on, years crawled past and I grew up.

Fast forward ...

As an adult, depression was a constant companion. After moving to New York in 1977, close friends would often receive late night phone calls from me when crushing fear and panic would take hold. These calls were my lifeline, my best way to cope. Friends would "talk me down" - sometimes for hours - until I could unhook from the panic and finally collapse, exhausted, into sleep.

This pattern continued for years.

When I moved to the West Coast in the late 1980's, however,

this fail-safe was undone. The three hour time difference meant I could no longer reach out to those friends. Any late night phone calls from me would have meant reaching out to friends at or after 1 or 2am there time. I love my friends but that three hour time difference meant I had to face and learn how to deal with my fears by myself.

Over the following years, I struggled, trying to find my footing, to make new friends and to broaden my network. I took esoteric spiritual and healing courses and learned useful methods to help myself through difficult times. From 1989 through the mid-1990's, I experienced several health crises and some challenging times in my fledgling career.

Crashing Waves: Disability and "ah ha" Moments

"Acceptance gives us the gift of resilience – fully joining the flow of life without being defined by what happens. As Maya Angelou said, "You may not control all the events that happen to you, but you can decide not to be reduced by them.""

– Sharon Salzberg,

Best selling author, teacher of Buddhist meditation practice,

Co-founder of Insight Meditation Society.

In 1989, I moved across the country and settled in beautiful Northern California. After some networking and landing a number of jobs through a temp agency, I became a freelance telemarketer. I'd had experience doing similar work as a volunteer in New York, so it seemed a good fit to take on professionally at this point. In early 1990 I decided to branch out and expand, so I began marketing myself as a telemarketing trainer as well. By the beginning of the summer of 1990, things were looking bright. There was the promise of steady work coming in and I had good friends to enjoy my time off with. Living in Marin County, California (just north of the Golden Gate Bridge), I would often travel across the bridges across the breathtakingly lovely San Francisco Bay to visit friends. The Accident happened on one of these trips in June or July of 1990. A car almost broadsided mine on the highway. The accident left me pretty banged up and unable to drive. I was fortunate that nothing was broken but I suffered terrible pain that lingered for weeks. I was stoic about it, though Things didn't seem so bad. I saw a chiropractor and dosed myself with aspirin and arnica, an old but effective herbal remedy for pain. But my recovery took longer than I expected. Not wanting to "be a burden", however, I didn't complain or let friends know what was happening. I rarely asked for help. I thought I had to take care of myself, be independent. If I asked for help, I thought people would see me as being weak. As if I wasn't, right? Weeks turned into months of "recovery", and my pain was constant. Depression, never far away in the best of times, descended on me like a thick fog. Its heaviness dragged me down, clouded my thinking and made sunshine-filled days seem gloomy and dark. As time passed, my frustration at my snails-paced recovery grew, deepening my depression and despair.

After several months of agonizingly slow recovery, one day I took a short walk through the nearby park. Dejected and discouraged, I found myself silently screaming at the Universe - "Why am I still in so much pain? Why aren't I better?" I was ready to give up and throw in the towel. I even seriously contemplated suicide. Deep in my despair, misery and physical pain, I felt that if life was going to continue this way – if my physical pain wasn't going to improve (and that's how it felt), why should I go on? At this point I had an eye-opening flash of insight. I realized there was nothing I could do to make my recovery go faster; I was already doing everything I could. The only thing left to do was to trust that my health support team – and Nature – would help me get better. I had to believe this was true, even with little evidence for it. It was at that moment, with that insight, that I finally let go of my expectations, of my demand of the Universe that I get better NOW. I slowly made my way home, where I made a simple dinner, read a little, then fell asleep. Amazingly, the next morning, my pain had lessened! And each following day it decreased even more. This unexpected miracle was, to me, an "ah ha" moment. I wondered: "Was giving up / letting go a key to getting better? Could it be that simple?"

That thought would come back to me throughout the coming years during times of crises, when depression seemed stronger than I was. Could letting go of the struggle, of the expectations, of the "I want it to\look / be the way I want it to look / be", be the key to regaining health and balance?

I discovered that in the face of depression, when everything seems blackest, there is a place within each of us that can be accessed to help dig ourselves out. Perhaps it begins with that thought – "let go!" This thought sustained me as I recovered and dove back into my life. As my energy returned, I looked ahead and eventually realized it was time for a big change. That included work, perspective AND where and how I lived.

After months of indecision and time spent looking for a new home in the country, in the spring of 1996, I left my home in the hills of Marin County and moved further north into a cozy cabin in a rural area surrounded by pastures and fields with a stunning view of Mt. Shasta, considered by many to be a sacred mountain. With a bubbling creek running through the property and surrounded by tall evergreens, it was an idealic place to live, one that fed my spirit and my soul.

But all was not peace and harmony. Shortly after moving into my comfy country cabin, I became very ill with what was eventually diagnosed as Chronic Fatigue. It was unlike any illness I'd experienced before. I suffered sudden frequent and severe energy loss, an inability to focus for long periods of time and lengthy bouts of depression. Months passed before I finally found a medical professional who could treat me and it took even longer before I was on the road to recovery.

Living alone in the country with barely any neighbors, I had to fend for myself. I lived a very solitary life, ate very little due to no appetite or inclination to cook, and had only the phone and my VCR to keep me connected or entertained.

My loss of energy was definitely intertwined with my depression. Without the former, I couldn't manage to avoid the latter. Depression became an all too frequent companion, resulting in long days and interminably long nights. During long months of slogging through constant exhaustion, sapped of strength, being unable to concentrate, I had hoped my family would be a source of solace. Sadly, during this time, my parents and I were at odds. They had no experience with this illness and didn't understand how I could be so debilitated that I couldn't work or even get around. This continuing discord added to my bouts of depression, which I had no stamina or strength to deal with.

During those difficult times, I knew I had to help myself any way I could. So I developed a mantra that I practiced daily. This was an unusual step for me; I generally wasn't one to follow such a practice. I would remind myself daily of the following:

> *"Look for 3 miracles every day.*
> *They can be as small as the sky is blue or the sun is shining.*
> *But always seek the miracles.*
> *Because they're there."*

I've since shared this mantra with friends and colleagues. It's simple to do and practicing it daily, particularly when going through challenging times, can make any burden a little easier to bear.

Back then, Chronic Fatigue was almost impossibly difficult to diagnose and even more so to treat. Many people suffer with it for years, some for a lifetime. I was incredibly fortunate to find a skillful health practitioner – Dr. James Said – so quickly. His treatments for my Chronic Fatigue– which included the use of numerous aromatherapy oils, chiropractic adjustments and other so called "alternative" healing modalities - worked. After going through an intense year of weekly treatments with Dr. Said, I am blessed to now live a life that's free of the debilitating suffering I experienced then.

Let's turn the focus on you for a moment. Have you ever had some circumstance of incident that left you unable to move forward? Something that stopped the action in your life for any length of time so that you had to regroup, rethink what you could do next? Take a moment and write this down below. You don't need all the details, just the bare bones of what happened.

....

....

....

....

....

....

Now take a moment and think back to that time What did you learn from having to "stop the action"? Was there a lesson or insight you gained from that? Write that down below. And be as specific as possible.

....

....

....

....

....

....

Very good. It's valuable to recognize these kinds of insights as they can often have a profound effect on our decisions and actions in the future.

For me, the insight that letting go could be a path to follow would prove useful – when I remembered it(! My illness wasn't the last such life test I'd confront. Over the years, health-related crises would arise again and again.

Chapter 3

Being a Pet Mom and Seeing the Mirror

"An effort made for the happiness of others lifts us above ourselves."

–Lydia M. Child

"If you light a lamp for somebody, it will also brighten your path."

– Buddha

Lots of people like riding roller coasters. I despise them. I hated them as a kid and don't like them as an adult. Yet my life has often felt like a giant roller coaster ride – taking me from emotional highs to frustrated lows, from dancing around in breathless exuberance to being dashed down to insomnia-causing anxiety and lingering chronic pain. Over the years, however, with a lot of hard work, introspection, meditation and support from friends, colleagues and mental health professionals, I've been able to level out those huge ups and downs.

Being a Pet Mom

Sometimes it feels like the roller coasters we're riding are traveling through long dark narrow tunnels. Believe me, I've ridden a few of those. One of these rides occurred with my fostering, then adopting my sweet, four-legged boy, my dog Magic. He was my companion and my best friend for almost 14 years.

I adopted Magic during a difficult time in my life. In 1997, I was living in a cabin in a somewhat remote area in Northern California surrounded mainly by cattle pastures and evergreens. My life was a solitary one – by choice. At that time, I was slowly recovering from Chronic Fatigue and had few friends or support to lean on. To ease my loneliness and to try to bring some balance to my life, I decided to seek out and adopt a dog. But I also had other reasons. A dog would be good protection, although there was almost no crime to speak of in my area, and I knew that having a dog would require me to get out of the house and walk every day, helping me to build my stamina and increase the rate of my recovery.

After months of research and phone calls to many S.P.C.A. shelters and rescue organizations throughout northern California, I found and rescued Magic, a one year old-ish blonde golden retriever-chow mix with a majestic curly plumed tail and a big smile.Magic came with plenty of baggage from the abuse he'd suffered through at the hands of his previous owners. He was him terrified of men and, I discovered, had no idea of how to deal with new situations. During the second week I'd had him, we went on a hiking trail that led up a small hill. On seeing someone coming down the hill towards us with a larger dog, the sight of that dog terrified Magic and he broke away from me, tearing down the hill at breakneck speed. Still in health recovery mode. I could only stumble slowly downhill after him, hoping he'd be at the bottom of the trail waiting for me.

Fearing the worst, I asked someone on their way up the trail if they'd seen him,. To my relief, they said a blonde dog had come streaking by but that he'd been secured by folks downhill and that he was waiting for me. Whew!!

As I was a fairly new "pet Mom", I hadn't had time yet to get him any special ID and he wasn't micro-chipped (foolish on my part). So I'd been terrified that in his terror-spurred run he'd just kept going and that I'd never see him again. You can bet that the next day we went to the pet store and I got a tag engraved with his name and my phone number on it, just in case anything like this happened again!

I spent many months helping Magic face his fears. I regularly took him places so he could meet new people and experience new environments and new situations. Each time he'd try to hide behind me but each time I'd tell him to "be brave" and would bring him out from behind me. Slowly he began to trust people I'd introduce him to and not shy away whenever we walked in our local park or down the street. Whenever he'd hesitate, I'd again tell him he could be brave and, steadily, he became braver.

It was so heartening to watch! It took much longer for him to be willing to trust men but slowly this evolved too. Over time, this frightened beautiful dog became a friendly, outgoing brave four-legged pal everyone loved.

Having Magic brought sweetness and light into my life. He was very smart, he learned quickly, he was independent-minded and funny. He always reminded me when I'd been working at the computer for a long time that it was time to stop and play. He was stealthy about that, though. I never saw it happen but at some point I'd look down and there, beside my chair, would be a toy or ball just waiting to be noticed. It always brought a grin to my face and I accepted the gentle but insistent nudge to get up and join in some fun.

As I grew stronger, Magic and I hiked many trails and the wilderness area around northern California. He always stayed on or near the trail, always kept me in sight. We had become a bonded pack. I never had to worry that he'd run off.

As Magic and I became closer, I observed his absolute joy of life and watched him letting go of his many deep fears. And I discovered something profound. Magic showed me that depression – that which I'd lived with all my life - can effect both humans AND animals. It was a real eye and mind opener.

Seeing the Mirror

In the year 2000, we were getting ready to move from our cabin in the country back to civilization - to Redding, California. After weeks of packing up boxes and making arrangements for the move, I began to notice Magic acting strangely. He was listless, glassy-eyed. He suddenly didn't want to eat or go for walks. Each day he would go out on our deck and just stand there, staring into space.

I was worried sick. What was going on with him? Had he gotten into something or perhaps eaten something poisonous? Suddenly a crazy thought flashed through my head.

Could it be that what I was seeing was depression?

I remembered that Magic was a rescue dog. He'd come from horrible situations with the worst abuse – three different former owners – all former police officers - had beat him, shot him, cursed and yelled at him and more. They'd clearly tried to train him to be a vicious dog, starting at age three months. All this I learned when I saw his medical records from the veterinarian who'd treated him through his entire life to that point. I discovered that he'd been treated for some kind of injury EVERY MONTH starting at three months and that no one had noticed this abuse. It was sickening to learn how Magic had suffered so with no one to help him. Then, to make things even worse, his former owners had completely given up on him and dumped him in a shelter in a high kill area – three different times! That he'd survived to reach me was a miracle. And an even bigger miracle was that his spirit hadn't been broken by all this horrendous treatment and abuse.

Magic and I had gone through a lot together to undo and heal the damage he'd lived with. With great love, gentleness and constant encouragement, he became happier, less fearful and more adventurous. I thought he'd come out the other side. But I hadn't realized he would react so intensely to the move. Clearly, if this was indeed depression he was experiencing and demonstrating, he must have felt he was going to be abandoned again, just as his other owners had done.

Acting on a hunch, I ran into the house and got a homeopathic remedy I personally used for trauma, upset or stress. In desperation, I gave him some of the tincture and waited to see what would happen.

And voila! My instincts were spot on. In a few moments, Magic "came back" to me. He wagged his tail again and relaxed. He was himself again. What a relief!

I learned something important that day. I finally SAW what my own depression must look like. My dog reflected back to me what others saw when I fell down the rabbit hole. That insight, that moment is clearly etched in my memory and has been a small but vital tool I draw on whenever I am tempted to fall down into that dark abyss. It's one of the many gifts my faithful friend gave me.

I could write a whole book about my life with Magic. We were a wonderful team. We played. We hiked. We shared time with good friends when we could. He brought joy and strength to my life where it had rarely been present before. While I taught him he was safe and secure, he taught me to be strong and courageous. Having him gave me confidence to go places and do things I'd rarely done before and to try new things. He was my other best half. Our bond was unbreakable.

It's time to turn the tables back to you. Here's a question:

Have you ever had a situation that's been like putting a mirror in front of you? For me, it was seeing Magic be depressed and realizing that's what I looked like. What was your mirror experience? Take a moment and write it down in the space below. Not the entire story, just the facts – what happened to show you it was a mirror? And be specific.

....

....

....

....

Okay. Now, using the space below, write down what you learned from that experience. Again, be specific.

....

....

....

....

....

....

Good work. It's useful to remember these kinds of situations and what you learned from them. These are building blocks that can help you in difficult situations you may face.

So let's go forward, shall we?

Chapter 4

Deeper Dives, Lessons, Opportunities and Choices

"When one door closes, another opens. But we often look so long and so regretfully at the closed door that we cannot see the one that has opened for us."

– Alexander Graham Bell

The tsunami of 1996 was but a mild storm compared to the next one that took place in the autumn of 1999. That one was a much deeper dive than before. It would be shake my life up and result in major life changes. And I never saw it coming.

Prior to the Fall of 1999, I was a freelance telemarketer working with clients in a variety of industries across the country. I was doing pretty well. I had a few clients; several articles I'd written were slated for publication and I was working on an exciting project that would take my writing career to the next big level. It looked like many of the goals I'd worked so hard to achieve were about to come true.

But that September everything changed.

On a sunny mid-September day, I was driving from my home in the country to Sacramento, California where I planned to catch a plane to go to a high school reunion. But the best laid plans have a way of going awry. As I reached the outskirts of Sacramento, someone drove where they shouldn't have and slammed into my car. It was a serious car accident. An ambulance rushed me to the hospital, Optimist that I was, I thought that it would only be a short time before I'd be back running my business (and my life) full tilt. False hope is tough to let go of.

But the Accident changed everything. Its aftermath left me unable to work or focus. I couldn't take care of myself; couldn't get around on my own. I was unable to run the simplest errand, unable to drive or do much of anything for months. It was devastating.

Following a brief stay in the hospital, I spent several days with friends in the Sacramento area, then a good friend drove down and took me back north. Realizing I was still weak and unable to fend for myself, I spent the next month at this friend's home in a small hamlet southwest of my cabin. My friend had been taking care of my dog Magic, ostensibly while I was off to my reunion. So my healing time also included nurturing from my four-legged friend.

While recuperating at my friend's, the most activity I could do was take short walks in the surrounding countryside. Nature has always been healing to me and these slow walks in the breathtaking beauty of the nearby hills lifted my spirit.

During my three-month convalescence, whether staying with friends or in an off-season tourist motel, I was in constant debilitating pain. Solitude – and my dog – were my close companions. Unable to care for myself, I depended on the kindness of friends – for running errands, grocery shopping, pretty much everything. All the while I yearned to be back at my cabin in the country, to be on my own again.

But in my weakened state – and perhaps because of it - I was also waging a recurring battle against depression. I was constantly fighting to not go over the edge – to stay out of the rabbit hole. And that was an almost impossible challenge when faced with the constant debilitating pain the accident had left me with.

Let me say here that I was raised to believe that if you worked hard and did all the right things, you'd reach your goals and dreams. I was taught that Life's ups and downs were just part of the ride.

But these circumstances were the most difficult of my adult life. Having been an active person before the Accident – one who jogged regularly, walked or hiked mountain and forest trails - "slow" became my new normal. I suddenly had to deal with new physical limitations. We all think debilitating illness or disaster won't happen to us. But it can and it does. When it happens, we're often unprepared for its impact. Simple things – like driving a car, opening heavy doors or lifting objects –become almost impossible. To be able to work, even to think straight, was a challenge. I learned plenty of "life lessons" from this experience - some of which I had to learn again at an even deeper level later in 2012.

The car accident forced me to face some tough questions. the answers to which would be critical. These included:

- If I told clients I couldn't do the job / project, or had to reschedule, would they understand? Or would I lose their business?

- With no clear "end" in sight, could I keep my business alive / in front of people so they didn't forget me - the old "out of sight, out of mind" thing?

- Was I being a burden to the people who were helping me?

- If my not being able to work for months continued, did that mean I wasn't contributing, not making a difference? This was one of my deepest fears.

As these questions swirled in my mind, my emotions careened towards panic and the vision of the depression pit loomed very close.

After my experience with illness and depression years before, when depression descended this time around, I knew I needed help. While staying at a vacant off-season tourist hotel owned by a friend, I contacted a mental health professional I'd recently been introduced to. We began meeting regularly so I could gain clarity about what was happening.

The work we did was often painful. Being by nature a private person, I was hesitant to share what was going on, much less examine what lay behind it all. Although my previous experience with Dr. Said had shown me that asking for help could make a profound difference, when it came to asking for help with a mental health professional, that was, in my mind, completely different. Asking for that kind of help didn't come naturally for me since, in my family, problems were kept private. That included not sharing troubles with therapists. There were times in our therapy sessions when I'd just sit there, practically immobilized for long periods, unable to speak. I discovered that good therapists allow patients to go at their own pace, even if that means letting them sit quietly while struggling to find what to say. Talking about my feelings, about my past, about how events and circumstances affected me at that point felt like torture.

But I believe what the poet John Dunne (and the old song) says is true: "No man (or woman) is an island." We all need people we can talk to/with. For me, finding this compassionate professional and learning to trust him was essential. He was literally a lifesaver.

As our work slowly progressed over many months,, I learned invaluable coping skills that would help me avoid going down the rabbit hole, or at least to not go so far down. Over time, I realized that choosing to work with a therapist was one of the best decisions I could have made. The skills and insights I gained from the work we did have served me well, enabling and empowering me through many difficult situations since then.

Lessons

One of the biggest lessons I've learned is that our most difficult challenges are what shape us, what make us stronger. If you neglect the lessons, you gain nothing from the ride. Embrace them and the fabric of your life – your tapestry - becomes much richer.

Here's some of what I learned from my experiences, from the aftermath of the Accident and from my work with my therapist.

- Letting go is important. If you keep trying to do things the way you used to or try to hang onto your past way of viewing things, you'll stay "stuck". Letting go frees you up to move forward, to consider new things or ideas and even perhaps to improve the quality of your life.

- People do want to help. I learned that helping people who are going through difficult times is a gift that enriches other peoples lives as well as our own, and if you ask for help, more times than not, you'll get it.

- Sitting still and resting are vital to recovery. But doing too much can set you back. You need to find a balance. Part of recovering from an accident like mine meant moving my body, getting out in Nature, breathing fresh air and getting some exercise. You don't recover without doing the work.

- Learning and practicing patience are critical and invaluable skills. For many of us (myself included), practicing patience is an exercise in itself. It can be as challenging as any physical therapy program. But its practice reveals new ideas and insights that help us gain a richer perspective of who we are and what we're capable of.

Opportunities

I discovered a lot of opportunities from this experience. That's right, even with the pain, frustration and my dashed hopes for a quick recovery, I discovered silver linings.

One was: when you are down and you open your heart, people reach out to help. Our relationships – be they professional or personal – are the foundation we count on during challenging times, they prop us up. The quality of those relationships shouldn't take a back seat to rushing around or to getting ahead in our careers. How we connect with others and the depth of those connections gives us the spirit and vitality we experience in life, which enriches our lives. Our interdependence, our interconnectedness is more important, more vital to the quality of our lives than our insistence on being independent.

The Accident – as traumatic, disruptive, and life altering as it was – had a real silver lining. I found out who my friends were. Their depth of caring and support often left me speechless. And very grateful. Discovering I have a net of love and support to count on might have been the Accident's greatest gift.

Let's turn this back your way for a moment. Turn to the back section of the book called Reflections to Ponder and find the poem "The Interconnectedness of our Lives". As you read through it, what does it bring to mind? Is there interdependence / interconnectedness in your life? Have you noticed this might be missing in some areas of your life? Would you like to experience more connection with others? What might this look like? Take a few moments to write your thoughts below.

....

....

....

....

....

Here's another question. What can you do, what actions can you take to create more connections to your life? It might mean taking a few small, simple steps – like reaching out to a friend you haven't spoken with in a long time or going to an event you might enjoy.

Write down at least 3 actions you can take to increase the interconnectedness in your life. Remember – be specific!

....

....

....

....

....

Good work. The road-map you're designing is beginning to take shape. Read on!

Chapter 5

Dancing Through an Ocean of Tears

Discovery

The greatest discovery of my generation is that human beings can alter their lives by altering their attitudes of mind.

— William James, 1842-1910

Experiencing trauma of any kind such as a loss or a serious injury can change how we react to things. A normally easy-going person can become someone who's frazzled, tense and short with people. Physical or emotional pain can be forerunners of depression; the worse the pain, the easier it is to slide into it. But it's important to know that as difficult as these times may be, they offer us significant lessons.

I have a confession to make. I've rarely kept a journal. That may sound odd coming from someone who's livelihood is writing.. But, in times of crisis - of deep pain and anguish – I've sometimes attempted to document my thoughts and feelings with the hope of being able to sort them out, to gain some clarity and resolution. The year between 1999 and 2000 was a period of tumultuous emotional roller coasters. During that time, I felt compelled to document my thoughts.

These are personal observations I wrote while I recuperated from the 1999 car accident I mentioned earlier. Although they may be a bit raw, they offer a glimpse into the despair and darkness I was dealing with as well as the glimmer of light I saw at the end of that tunnel.

#1

Everyone – my doctor, my physical therapist, my chiropractor, even my massage therapist – says the same thing: "Be gentle with yourself." Even my walking partner tries to be encouraging. They mean well and are trying to be supportive. But even just the idea of being kind or gentle with myself while going through such pain is almost impossible to accept.

#2

I've come a long way over these past weeks. I can finally walk without that awful limp and can even walk as much as two to five miles every few days – occasionally even power walking. Sometimes I'll include some light jogging, but only on dirt trails, since jogging on pavement can still mess up my neck and back.

I think I'm doing terrific - until things flare-up or until I try some new movement, or I try to be a little more active than usual.

When I try to do simple but slightly strenuous tasks, "stuff" hits the proverbial fan. Suddenly the pain hits me again and I bounce from deep depression to frustration to burning anger and back again.

#3

Once again someone said: "You're still recovering from the accident." WHAM!! "How long," I screamed silently, "until I'm fully recovered? How long is this going to take? What can I do to climb out of this pit?"

Platitudes, the "nice" phrases people say to reassure me – they make me want to jump out of my skin! Things like "You're in the home stretch." Or "just be patient. You've come a long way already." And then there's: "It takes as long as it takes." When I hear these, I want to shriek or throw something to vent my frustration and anger.

"Enough", I sometimes yell at my friends, my doctors, even at at the universe. "Enough!"

#4

It's been well over a month now. Isn't it time to be recovered, to take my life on fully again? I'm desperate to take things for granted. again. I daydream of being on the go without suddenly becoming drained of energy and having to stop.

I want to drive down to the (San Francisco) Bay Area on a whim to visit friends, or burn the candle at both ends again and not have to deal with the repercussions I know will hit me if I do. But all I can do is wait for my recovery to run its course. And I AM NOT KNOWN FOR MY PATIENCE!

#5

Depression can pursue you, quietly creeping up 'til it grips you by the throat when you least expect it. During these tough months, I've often sensed a shadow behind me. It would suddenly, inexplicably catch me off guard and send me plummeting downward. I never knew when It would hit, but It was always there, skulking in the background, ready to pounce at any moment.

#6

I hate to admit it but I was a Victim. Too often I felt I was being yanked along, with no ability to stop it. I'd forgotten I had leverage over what was happening. It's easy to become a Victim without realizing it. At those times, being able to act any other way is an alien concept. You're on a narrow, one-way road and you can't see anything else.

Now let's flash forward.

By mid-2000, I had regained my health and mobility and dove into rebuilding my business – and my perspective. Over the course of my long recovery, I'd gotten used to living with pain and it took some time for me to reclaim my ability to think of myself as fully recovered. But reclaim it I did and life flowed smoothly forward again.

But as my life's pattern showed again and again, the rare smooth times were frequently book ended by emotional upheaval.

The following observations come from those times. These were made before and right after my depression was diagnosed. I've edited some places for clarity.

From January 2000 during a two day emotional "letting go"

I finally call it what I've suspected it was: Depression comes crashing in huge waves, with some little distance between them. I never know when the next one will appear and cascade over my head. Each one "hits" my body as an intense physical force.

Initially it seems like the onset of illness. Not until I am well into it do I recognize this emotional tsunami just as the next wave crashes over me. Until now, I've only experienced depression's milder form. This is a scary time.

I have the classic signs - the sudden, inexplicable sobbing, grief that lays me flat on the floor, moaning with deep emotional pain. Is this latest wave from the healing session I recently went through or has this built-up from the stress and upset I've been enduring? Could this be the sadness and grief of separation from someone not meant to be part of my life, or could the Accident and its life-altering ramifications be a part of this?

My Wants

But does the cause really matter? Surviving each emotional wave I find myself on is the most difficult task I've faced so far. Writing about it and my woefully meager meditation practice help to give me a glimmer through the waves of what balance could be, though not enough for me to reach out and grab hold of it. Looking For A Label?

Not understanding what's happening is tough. What do I call this – somebody give me a label please! I've always looked for labels; which is ironic, since I've always shunned labels when others tried to apply them to me.

Am I Drowning?

I need to find something I can understand, a lifesaving rescue ring I can hold onto and use to not drown. My emotions are like crashing waves caused by an ocean storm, endlessly battering the sandy beach while throwing ocean debris on the shore. We cannot stop the waves from crashing. We can only embrace the rhythm and hope to find a loving hand stretched our way to help us jump those waves.

We hope for rescue from pain or distress but most of us aren't willing to get to the bottom of whatever's happening. So this tsunami - is it finally reaching high tide and about to crash onto the shore, leaving behind its flotsam and the need to regroup for what's next? There is hope. But I recognize that it may take months for the silver lining to reveal itself.

Months crawled by. I somehow regained some of my equilibrium, yet felt I was operating "over the top" as I went through my daily life. But there was more emotional upheaval to come.

From November 2 & 3, 2000, finally facing the reality of another failed relationship

Once again, grief paralyzes and envelopes me. I can only sit and sob uncontrollably. I grieve for the lost child that will never be, for the promising relationship that never fully materialized and that I feared the most. I grieve for time lost and for things I've pushed away. Even when the grief is at bay, I feel weak, spent, unable to do anything other than sit and stare at nothing.

There have already been years worth of grieving. Will there ever be an end, or must this tidal wave of heart-wrenching grief and sadness continue to crash through my life? Sometimes it's clear for whom or what I grieve. Other times, it's like the murky shore's edge – you know it's there but it's mostly hidden. Buddhism refers to the kind of deep sadness I've going through the "Great Grief" - for which there is no clear identifying or delineation.

I've tried meditation to gain some relief or clarity but it hasn't alleviated the downward spiral into the vortex which blots out the sun and draws me into the depths. Where is the rainbow – with its colorful glory – that's supposed to shine through this ocean of tears? A thundering roar constantly, relentlessly shouts at me. FAILURE ruthlessly tumbles me into the tsunami. My mind screams:

"You aren't being consistent.
You've failed because you said "no" to the child you'll never have;

because you run away when you get close to having what you've always wanted;

because you can't handle things yourself and you have to call other people to help."

But there is no mercy here. So the once small voice now broadcasts thunderously out to the heavens in an agonizing loop:

"You Are a Failure!
And you'll keep on being a Failure,
no matter what you do or how hard you try!

How can I survive with this loud, abrasive, obnoxious and deeply hurtful voice? Will there ever be a way to survive this or a way to go beyond this tsunami?

Post Script: Reflections from Today

I never wanted to write any of this down. Clearly, that's why it's taken me well over a decade to gather all my notes and rantings together and put them into what you're reading now.

Reading through what I've written tears at my heart. Looking back and with the hindsight and wisdom gained from the passage of time, I see how completely lost I was.

As I've reviewed that two-day emotional "letting go" that took place in November 2000, and its revelations, and as heart wrenching as it was to go through, I have discovered how cathartic it was. It forced me to recognize my deepest fears, ones I'd been hiding from, refusing to confront. For too many years I'd buried my emotions. By facing up to my fears and emotions, I finally saw the truth behind them, which gave me the strength and confidence to move forward. When you accept the truth behind your fear and allow yourself to go down into the deep murky muck, you'll discover treasure there. Those treasures will help you face future demons that dare to come calling. We cannot allow fear to stop us from living the full, creative life we were meant to live. If we cringe and shy away from the pain and fear, fear wins and we lose. Let's pause a moment. Take a look at the quote at the beginning of Chapter 1. Eleanor Roosevelt was married to perhaps one of the greatest U.S. Presidents in history, one who faced and overcame large personal obstacles while steering a country through numerous national crises. As his wife, Mrs. Roosevelt was intimately familiar with facing fears and doubts. Most biographies depict Eleanor Roosevelt as a young, shy, awkward woman. Many don't know she served as her husband's eyes and ears, as his outspoken partner, traveling and fact finding for him. This enabled the President to make difficult decisions of national importance.

Eleanor Roosevelt did not let fear or doubt stop her. She knew that to do so would have too high a cost.

Okay. It's your turn again. Think a moment, then write down three things – situations and/or circumstances – where you've let fear stop you. No judgment here. Just make a short list. Be specific – don't let yourself off the hook!

....

....

....

....

Now let's look a little deeper. What could you accomplish if you didn't let those fears stop you? Are there things you could achieve that would make you proud of yourself in a way you've always wanted? Write at least three things down and, again, be specific!

....

....

....

....

....

....

....

In life, courage is vastly different than what we see in the movies. Courage isn't acting without fear. It's the flip side. Courage is being willing to face your fear and to step through it – using that fear to brace you as you move forward. Every time you do this, you gain a little more confidence and skill to do it again. And each time, it gets a little easier. Having the courage to face our fears – to take them with us – creates the possibility for us to reach our dreams in life, and the opportunity for us to experience joy.

Chapter 6

Expectations and Rabbit Hole Revelations

The greatest discovery of my generation is that human beings can alter their lives by altering their attitudes of mind.

--William James

In 2005, I once again went down the rabbit hole. That year I found myself in an unhealthy relationship with a charismatic, charming man. Unbeknownst to me, he was also very narcissistic. As our relationship developed, I found our interactions and conversations would pivot often without warning from sweet to cruel and back again,. I'd had no experience with someone like this so I had no clue how to deal with the tumultuousness. Finally, to help regain my sense of balance and well-being, I ended the relationship.

Foolishly, however, I chose to stay in touch with this man. And, not surprisingly, one evening, a long phone conversation with him went very badly. Once again, the yo-yo swung from sweet flowing words to cruelty occurred, pivoting so suddenly it was breathtaking. This sudden swing had a devastating effect on me, triggering me into a downward emotional spiral that led to a deep rabbit-hole depression.

I knew I was in trouble, so I reached out by phone to a couple of good friends from nearby Mt. Shasta. My depression was so intense I could barely speak. Words stuck in my throat. Even breathing was difficult.

After a brief conversation with my friends, I did the next natural thing to me. Being a writer, I tried writing down what was going on – to express my thoughts and feelings, to make sense of the emotions that were bubbling up. It was, for me, the logical thing to do. Yet scribble as I might, my thoughts were jumbled and made no sense. I gained none of the clarity I'd sought.

Later, after a second phone call with my friends, they grew concerned for my well being. They got in their car, drove for over an hour and showed up at my house - and brought the 41 police with them. My friends pleaded with me to open the door, to let them and the police in so that they could speak with me. They grew more and more concerned.

For over an hour I resisted anyone coming in the house. I huddled in a corner of my kitchen, clinging to my dog, and tried to shut my ears to the pleas of those on the other side of the front door. During that very tense hour, I kept trying to phone and reach a good friend of mine. Numerous times I'd call, only to be told he wasn't available to talk. The more times I called and was told this, the deeper my despair became. He was my lifeline and I couldn't catch it. Over the course of six or seven unsuccessful phone calls to him, the black cloud of my pain and desperation grew and I went further down the rabbit hole.

Finally, after what seemed like an eternity with me unable to reach my friend and still unwilling to open the front door to my friends, the police broke the door in. My friends were relieved that I was alright, that I hadn't tried to do anything to hurt myself, but, to be on the safe side, the police took me to the emergency room to get help. There truly are times we need qualified help to sort the big things out and this was one of them.

After being led to an examining area in the emergency room and waiting alone there for several hours, a doctor finally arrived. After checking me out, he gave me several options. I could either be checked into the hospital for a 72 hour observation "hold", or to go where someone could keep me under observation. I chose to go to a nearby Buddhist monastery where I'd previously attended spiritual retreats and where I knew the monastic community. I knew I would be safe there. And it was near the beautiful sacred mountain Mt. Shasta, so I knew I'd be able to draw peace and solace from it as well.Over the course of the next few days, I rested and meditated. I also met several times with one of the monks to discuss what was going on with me. As the days passed, I slowly felt a bit of equilibrium returning although it was clear that restoring balance in my life would take time. But the quiet contemplation and counseling I received while at Shasta Abbey were healing to my battered spirit and were essential factors that helped me climb out of the dark hole I'd been trapped in.

Going through difficult circumstances always offer us invaluable lessons. What I learned from this incident was that holding on and having an expectation that people would change had driven me to this emotional tailspin. You cannot hold on to hoping someone will change how they are. False hope leads to disappointment and, in my case, despair. People are who they are and repeatedly do what they do. Wanting it or them to be different won't make it so.

As an adult, I've often had to re-learn the same big lesson: circumstances change; people almost never do. Nothing stays the same and people don't change their behavior even if we hope they will. There ARE rare exceptions, of course, but that's where we get into trouble – expecting that this time was the exception. This realization has helped me through many difficult times. Knowing there's always a way out of the rabbit hole buoys my spirits. It's another key to helping me stay out of depression.

Now, when things get tough or disappointments happen – and, let's face it, in life they often do – with the therapy and counseling I've done over the years, the techniques I've learned help me lift myself out of depression before I become entrenched in it. I know what to watch for and the actions I need to take. I've learned to trust that I'll act in my own best interest in those moments.

Like many of us, I was raised to believe I should be able to handle things on my own. A ridiculous idea, by the way. I've learned that seeking help, seeking counsel from people qualified to give it and learning how to help yourself, are vital elements that can help you through even the most difficult, emotion-laden times.

The truth is, NO ONE makes it on their own, by themselves, without help from someone somewhere. Life just doesn't work that way. Balance in our lives comes through connecting with others. Reaching out, getting the support you need and learning necessary life skills you can use to keep yourself from falling down the rabbit hole are essential tools that can help you bring balance back into your life.

Alright, time to take a look at your own perspective.

We all have expectations – of ourselves, of others. Take a moment and look at the people in your life, especially those you're closest with – good friends, colleagues, loved ones. Are there expectations you have that they haven't met, possibly can't meet? Are you expecting or hoping someone in your life will change over time? Use the space below to write at least three examples of this. Be specific – you don't have to name names; just list enough so you'll know who it is. And clearly state the expectation you have.

....

....

....

....

....

Alright. Now take a moment and write down how those expectations NOT being met effect you? When they do or don't do "x", you feel "y", that kind of thing. The answers may be pretty revealing.

....

....

....

....

....

....

What did you learn from doing this exercise? You may begin to see that your unfulfilled expectations can well be a trigger for you heading towards your personal rabbit hole. I know that's true for me. When you can recognize this, there's the opportunity for an 'ah-ha" moment of your own.

So let's move forward, shall we?

Chapter 7

Depression's Nuts, Bolts and Surprising Links

"Depression ... is that absence of being able to
envisage
that you will ever be cheerful again.

The absence of hope. Sad hurts, but it's a healthy
feeling.
It is a necessary thing to feel. Depression is very
different."

---JK Rowling

"Depression is a flaw in chemistry not character."
---from HealthyPlace.com

We who live with depression periodically fall victim to it. At times that feels like "Oh, God, here it is again," usually followed by "Why aren't I done with this yet?"

Some of the most talented, gifted people have suffered from depression: Sylvia Plath, Soren Kierkegaard, Ernest Hemingway, JK. Rowling, Lady Gaga and Dwayne "The Rock" Johnson,to name a few. I'm not arrogant enough to put myself on the same page that these eminent artists, authors and actors occupy. But living with depression? I am intimately familiar with what that means.

To help get a handle on understanding and dealing with depression's symptoms and repercussions, I've sought counseling at various times from qualified professionals.

There's no shame in reaching out and seeking support. This perspective probably saved my life more than once. The work I did with my therapist from 2000 to 2003, for example, was challenging. occasionally painful, yet always helpful. I gained bushels full of insights and strategies from those therapy sessions. Here are a few.

- When you're "stuck" - in whatever position you find

- yourself, be it on the floor or wherever – get up and move! This kind of distraction by movement can help you avoid going over the edge.

- Dance! You can't be depressed when you're dancing! (And it's very difficult to frown while you're dancing too!)

- Learn to make distinctions. Lumping everything together– emotions, moods, decisions – isn't constructive but it can be destructive.

- Feeling "blue" and being depressed are very different. Prior to being in therapy, I hadn't known what feeling "blue" – feeling a bit down but not so deep that you're depressed – meant. And when I finally did understand it, I was stunned that I I could make that choice! When all you've ever known has been either being depressed or not, a third, milder option like "blue" is a shocker.

Depression is a big, important topic. Doing it justice in this book hasn't been an easy task.

To gain a deeper perspective, I circled back to my former therapist to discover some of the nuts and bolts of what I'd been living and dealing with. There were definitely some surprises in store. The following is excerpted from interviews with John Cunningham, the Marriage and Family Therapist I'd worked with in Northern California. As you read through this section, consider how you might best use this information in your daily life.

"Clinical depression is unique to each person," says Cunningham. "Everyone experiences it differently. "Depression takes many forms. What are they and how do they differ?

Cunningham talks about "the depression zone." The symptoms of depression, he said, range from obsessive thinking, to ruminating, to a mood disorder that has you down in the dumps, to a type of emotional cycling where the mood impairs thinking which impairs the mood (I relate to the latter).

The National Institute of Health (NIH) expands on this list of symptoms. Reading through this, it is important to remember many people with depression may only experience one or two of these symptoms. Also, the NIH stresses that to be diagnosed with depression, the symptom must be present for at least two weeks. Symptoms that seem similar but are shorter-lived are are probably not depression.

The NIH expanded symptom list includes:

- Persistent sad, anxious, or "empty" mood

- Feelings of hopelessness, or pessimism / irritability

- Feelings of guilt, worthlessness, or helplessness

- Loss of interest or pleasure in hobbies and activities

- Decreased energy or fatigue

- Moving or talking more slowly

- Feeling restless or having trouble sitting still

- Difficulty concentrating, remembering, or making decisions

- Difficulty sleeping, early morning awakening, or oversleeping

- Appetite and/or weight changes

- Thoughts of death or suicide, or suicide attempts

- Aches or pains, headaches, cramps, or digestive problems without a clear physical cause and/or that do not ease even with treatment

The NIH also breaks down the different types of depression. [1] These include:

- Persistent depressive disorder (also called dysthymia)

A person diagnosed with persistent depressive disorder may have episodes of major

---

1   National Institute of Mental Health website https://www.nimh.nih.
48   gov/health/topics/depression/index.shtml

depression along with periods of less severe symptoms, but symptoms must last for two years to be recognized as persistent depressive disorder.

- Seasonal Affective Disorder (SAD)

This disorder is characterized by the onset of depression during the cold winter months, when there's less natural sunlight. The depression generally lifts during spring and summer.

Winter depression, an apparent subset of SAD, is typically accompanied by social withdrawal, increased sleep, and weight gain –and it predictably returns every year in seasonal affective disorder.

- Psychotic depression – a person has severe depression plus some form of psychosis, such as having disturbing false fixed beliefs (delusions) or hearing or seeing upsetting things that others cannot hear or see (hallucinations)

The psychotic symptoms typically have a depressive "theme," such as delusions of guilt, poverty, or illness.

- Bipolar disorder.

This differs from clinical depression. People with this experience both low moods and extreme high – as in euphoric – or irritable moods called "mania" or a less severe form called "hypo mania."

As you consider these, try not to get caught up in labels. It's a lot more productive to recognize what's true for you and move forward from there. As a society, clinical depression is far more prevalent in all its forms than we care to admit. But too often this illness is seen as a character flaw rather than a physiological disorder.

Once you enter into a clinically depressive state, says Cunningham, you have a neurochemical, biological issue, just like you would have with diabetes, hypothyroidism or high blood pressure. Cunningham says that anxiety appears to be one of the most common manifestations of depression, just like sleep disturbance is. And – this may surprise you – the presence of depression carries a strong genetic link that can effect family members.

But one can be anxious or have a "bummer" mood and not be depressed, he said. However, situational events can kick an underlying depression into high gear.

The trap, says Cunningham, is we try to pick a symptom or an idea like "If I can only feel better" or "If I can only think better, then my depression would go away," rather than recognizing that the mood disorder, the cognitive obsessing looping disorder and the anxiety disorder are the symptoms - "the expression of something much more important" - biology.

We have to deal with the biology of the issue and address it from that perspective rather than (from) the mood of the issue, said Cunningham. And by biology, he means focusing on the body, doing activities like walking, working out, dancing, meditation (somatic meditation, rather than just watching thoughts), even yoga. You (need to) give your mind something to do relative to your body, says Cunningham, even if it's just observing, watching your breathing, your mood shifts.

Now here's where surprises start tumbling around. Cunningham says most people get caught up in addictions of some form when attempting to deal with their mood disorder or issues. It's easier to self-medicate, he said, than to face uncomfortable feelings like sadness, hopelessness, feeling numb, feeling isolated, etc. that come with being depressed. Substance abuse, he said, is a secondary diagnosis for an underlying depression a significant percent of the time.

[2]The Integrated Treatment of Substance Abuse & Mental Illness website says this Dual Diagnosis happens over 50 percent of the time. Cunningham ranks that figure much higher - close to 100 percent! "That's an extreme example of people trying to alter mood," said Cunningham. "They end up in (physical) addiction, which spins the depression deeper because it impairs sleeping."

There are other forms of addiction as well – food, sugar, video games, porn – mood shielding / altering things. Have you used any of these to stave off feeling depressed? All too often, food and sugar have been my best friends.

"Anything mood altering can be addictive," said Cunningham "(And) though not all addictions are harmful, they're still addictions," he said. And, as we know, our culture stigmatizes depression as well as addictions. Sadly, many consider having depression – and admitting to it – shameful. This can make us hide depression from others as well deny it in ourselves. This can show up in various ways. For example, for years, I'd been cautious when filling out medical forms. When a form asked if I have depression or anxiety, I was more likely to check the latter than the former for fear that insurance companies might "ding" me for my honesty. Fortunately, they can no longer ask this question.

"In a sense," said Cunningham,"like heart disease, it's a silent killer."Those who suffer from undiagnosed depression may appear "normal" to neighbors, friends and community members.

Yet what's churning underneath can be excruciating and devastatingly painful – even fatal. Cunningham told of a family friend who inexplicably and tragically took his and his wife's life and left a family in disbelief and grieving. The poem Cunningham wrote - - "The Impenetrable Veil" - acknowledges the tragedy of depression. "It's the hidden veil no one could cross," he said

Excerpt from "The Impenetrable Veil" by John Cunningham
Used by permission

"A parent's worst nightmare is to bury their own child.Few admit to fighting the fears of your child's mental illness,

A debilitating powerlessness of immobility and rejected assistance.

The hidden silence of mental illnessmoves blindto the facts of love,affection, sacrifice,joy, dreams, and celebration."

The build-up to this tragedy was a hidden veil that no one could cross, said Cunningham. Yet, he said, it's just another medical problem. Viewed from this perspective – that this is a biological health issue – dealing with depression, in whatever form it takes, can be a little easier.

Another important factor interwoven with triggering depression is when it's triggered by a chemical reaction. There is evidence that gut health and digestion are inextricably linked to well-being. There is a distinct connection between[3] the health of our gut and our digestion and the brain. Evidence shows that poor gut health is involved with depression and anxiety. An imbalance in our microbiome - the diverse population of microbes (bacteria) that live in our gastrointestinal (GI) tract – can be associated with inflammation and can be linked to illnesses such irritable bowel syndrome (IBS), celiac disease and others.

I've tried to keep the technical stuff to a minimum here but I think at this point a little technical stuff will help.

There are several neurotransmitters – those chemical messengers that carry, boost and balance signals between neurons (nerve cells) and cells throughout the body. One such neurotransmitter called serotonin helps[4] relay signals from one area of the brain to another. Serotonin is manufactured in the brain BUT at least 90 percent is found in the digestive tract Researchers believe that an imbalance of serotonin can lead to depression, anxiety, obsessive-compulsive disorder, panic, even excess anger. Unfortunately there currently is no way to measure the levels of serotonin in the brain so there are no studies on this. However, blood levels of serotonin are measurable and have been shown to be lower in people who suffer from depression. Antidepressants categorized as SSRIs (selective serotonin reuptake inhibitors) and SNRIs (serotonin and nonrepinephrine inhibitors) are believed to reduce symptoms of depression, though how they actually work isn't fully understood. A great deal more can be said about the body-mind connection, but that may be for another book, not this one. Suffice to say that the mind, the body and the spirit are intricately connected. If even one is out of balance, it affects our well-being. Balance, then, is yet another key factor to be aware of.

---

3   "The Gut Brain Connection: How Gut Health Affects Mental Health', by Susan McQuillan, MS, RDN. . https://www.psycom.net/the-gut-brain-connection

4   "Serotonin: 9 Questions and Answers" by Colette Bou chez. WebMD; https://www.webmd.com/depression/features/serotonin#1

That's a lot to digest, isn't it? Let's break it down a little, make it a bit more personal.

Think about what you've just read. Now, using the space below, make a list of at least 3 things you've discovered or learned so far, ideas that might be useful tools for you the next time you're standing at the edge of your own abyss.

....

....

....

....

Now, if you were to use these tools, are there other steps, even small ones, you would need to take to help you find your path back to balance? This is about possibilities. There is no "right answer" here. Consider this as a "what if I knew" perspective and then write down what comes up. And be as specific as possible!

Steps

....

....

....

....

....

....

....

....

....

....

....

Good work! You've made a great start to creating a useful road map for yourself. More on this as we go. As you go forward through the rest of this book, I encourage you to bear something else in mind.

Living with depression, in those moments of clarity when we can step outside the morass – the entangled mess we often find ourselves in - we long to burst the bubble of our emptiness, our sadness. We want to move on, full steam ahead. But we can't seem to figure out how. But with what you've just written down, you've begun to identify what might help you in those moments.

There's one universal truth we must recognize: We cannot move forward until we're able to acknowledge, recognize and accept where we are NOW. That is the starting point from which we walk forward – to help ourselves move up and out of the rabbit hole and into a more balanced life.

So keep reading for more useful nuggets!

Chapter 8

Being Tough Ain't What It's Cracked Up to Be: Mis-Perceptions Revealed and Depression's Gifts

Living Life
Come to the Edge, Life said.
They said, "We are Afraid."Come to the Edge, Life said. They Came.Life Pushed Them.And They Flew.-

Guillaume Apollinaire, 1870 - 1918

Throughout my life, I thought you had to be "tough" on the outside to succeed. As an adult living in New York City, I'd participated in a number of transformational programs. Among the many lessons those programs taught me, I learned that making things happen in my life was up to me, that I had to do whatever it took to accomplish something, even if it meant doing it myself.

There's clearly a downside to living this way. When things didn't go well, when there were difficulties or when I was ill or got hurt, I would suck it up and keep going – because I was tough. That mindset stemmed from childhood, where I constantly heard: "people don't really care. They don't want to know."My inclination had always been to share how I felt with others. But my parents continually drummed the notion of "they don't care" into me. This went against all my instincts.

It overrode my natural tendency to include others in order to find solutions to problems I was facing and reinforced the belief of needing to be tough. It took years before I finally learned that most people really DO care, that they want to be supportive.

Ideally, being supportive is a two-way street – a give and take. I've always been good at supporting people – giving moral support, lending an ear, being sympathetic. But when it came to me asking for support, that was different. I often wound up carrying a lot of "stuff" on my already burdened shoulders. The exceptions took place when I was desperate, particularly during the 1980's on those long panicky nights in New York when I felt forced to reach out to friends. Desperation can make you do things you normally wouldn't do.

Not letting others "in" to help ease my burden had a price. It took the form of health issues and accidents that left me effectively disabled. Through these distressing times, depression was always present, never fading. Yet, over the years, as I learned to finally face my fears, I also discovered the importance of patience and the powerful role letting go played. But these lessons took a great deal of time to finally sink in.

As I discussed in Chapter 3, I had a serious car accident in 1999. This, plus 2005's failed relationship and subsequent severe depression, brought me some surprises and some new opportunities to learn from.

Mis-Perceptions Revealed & Depression's Gifts

Every "crisis", every struggle we go through, offers us gifts. I know. That may sound corny or cheesy, but it's really true. These "gifts" may include:

- increased understanding of what is real versus what we perceive to be true

- a deepening of our ability to recognize what's going on around us

- accepting that it's okay to reach out and ask for help

- even being able share with others in our life (loved ones, close friends) more of the   inner struggle we've been engaged in.

"Gifts" can always be found in the midst of adversity. We may not recognize them at first. But they're always there if we're willing to look for them.

I want to expose and debunk a popular misconception many of us are raised with: that we have to "make it on our own". A story I was told a few years ago about my father illustrates this misconception perfectly.

My Dad was an extraordinary man. In many respects, we were very much alike – stubborn, determined and inclined to hold our ground on any issue once we made up our minds. Not surprisingly, we often disagreed about things which distanced us from each other for long stretches of time.

Viewed as a successful, self-made man, family stories about my dad were often repeated about how, to avoid his older brother's plans to set the course of my father's life, Dad enlisted in the Navy. Later, he enrolled in, and attended, the University of Texas at Austin for both undergrad and law school. Ultimately he established and built a successful law firm.

When I started my first business venture, I went to Dad for guidance. Sadly, he admitted he had little to offer me. Instead, he stressed that I must plug away, work hard and keep going until I made it. The impression I was left with was: I was on my own.

Years later, a close family friend told me tales of my Dad's early years in business. Turns out he struggled a lot in the early days. He and one of his close friends spent a lot of time at the Rexall drugstore food counter which, by the way, made the best hamburgers in the world and served amazingly delicious fountain Cokes. These two friends would sit and discuss and worry about their fledgling businesses and wonder whether or not they would succeed. This was something my Dad never shared with his kids, at least not with me.

My friend said that after some time, a leader in the community reached out and hired Dad to help him, mentoring him and sending business his way. This mentoring really helped Dad build his business and led him to become the successful and influential presence people knew.

So what was my take-away from this story? Simply that NO truly successful person EVER does it alone. Someone is always there to support him / her along the way. And it's often more than one person.

The notion that to succeed we have to do it on our own can lead to despair, isolation and depression. And it's just plain nonsense. A more positive interpretation of the notion that we must go it alone is that we must adjust our way of thinking and break free from the mindset we were raised with. This can be done.

Throughout my life's journey, I often found myself locked in depression, standing alone. That hasn't served me – nor you, the reader, I suspect. Reaching out to others, not standing alone, letting friends and/or colleagues know we need encouragement and allowing ourselves to receive it – that's what allows us the chance to move forward again. Choosing to be open and vulnerable can be scary – and it may go against the way you were raised to think or act – but it's the recipe for embracing life and relating with others.

Okay. Now let's look at some of YOUR ideas and thinking.

What are some notions you grew up believing that actually came from others, ideas that weren't true for you? List at least three of them in the space below. Be specific!

....

....

....

....

Too often we've taken on other people's points of view or mindsets of who we should be, of what we can or can't do. Because they allegedly "knew better" or because we believed them, we abandoned our instincts, our gut feelings of what our "right direction" was. As a result, we've often walked a path we weren't meant to follow. When we can let go of those well-meaning but frequently misguided suggestions about how we are "expected" to do things and the more we are true to ourselves, the less likely we are to stumble into that deep rabbit hole.

As I've traveled along my own path, I've learned how important and valuable it is to have a support team. The "no man is an island" thing is very true. However there was one avenue of support that I resisted for a long time. That was taking medication for my depression. For years I mistakenly thought that taking antidepressants would made me weak. I couldn't have been more wrong. Antidepressants are an invaluable tool for someone living with depression. It can mean the difference between living an active, engaged life and struggling through, or slogging through, as I like to call it.

My resistance to taking meds went back to how I was raised – the notion that I had to be able to handle my own problems without help. Remember that one? Well, after much soul searching and talking with close friends, I finally surrendered to the idea that medication could be helpful, that it wouldn't make me weak but instead it could help me become more balanced, more centered.

Finding the correct medicine and the proper dosage doesn't happen overnight. For me, this quest took months, a lot of patience (never my strong suit!) and some very uncomfortable trial and error before we discovered what worked. But it was worth it. Once we found what worked and I began taking the medication daily, it felt like the sun shone brighter and a huge weight fell off my shoulders – one I didn't even know I'd been carrying!

Reverend Seikai Luebke, a Buddhist monk I know in Northern California who has dealt with depression his entire life, said it well in his book **Depth Spirituality: Buddhism in the Age of Desire:**

"The deepening of my practice showed me that I need to make use of anything which can relieve human suffering, and if that means taking an antidepressant, then that's a good thing to do. ... that antidepressant is nothing short of miraculous in itself. And ... I've witnessed that illness has much to teach people about what's important in life." [5]

When my doctor and I landed on the right medication, my life opened up. It was then that I was finally able to tap into my creativity, discover joy and feel fully alive. Rediscovering my love of writing and my decision to pursue it as a career path is, I believe, a direct result of incorporating the right antidepressant into my life. Medication became a powerful resource for me – and it may be for you if that's the direction you take. Whatever path you choose, the support of a strong Wellness Team is vital for you to become and stay successful on your journey.

I've learned it's crucial to delve as deep inside as possible to discover what is true for me, and then follow that path. It doesn't always come easy for me. Far from it. But doing this work – despite what others think – is one way I help myself stay out of the pit. Not doing this essential work can cause me great suffering.

I used to think that being stoic was the way to deal with depression – to tough it out. It's not. We can't just tough our way to good mental health; we have to work at it. Allowing others in, beyond that facade of toughness, helps us reach the balance we all seek. Interacting with others, developing and utilizing our support network – these are what allow us to design a satisfying,

---

5 Luebke, Seikai Reverend, Depth Spirituality: Buddhism in the Age of Desire; Fausset Printing for Pine Mountain Buddhist Temple; published 2017.

successful and balanced life.

The 17th century poet John Dunne said it well:

> *"No man is an island, entire unto himself, ...*
> *Because I am involved in mankind,"*

So where do we go from here? Let's delve deeper and see what we can discover.

Chapter 9

Still Gotta Long Way to Go: Grief and Loss Take Center Stage

True Bravery

"You're braver than you believe, You're stronger than you seem, And smarter than you think."

– Christopher Robin to Pooh Bear

Life has its ups and downs and for someone who lives with depression, during times of health crises, depression gets worse, sometimes becoming chronic. Grief can trigger depression too. Grief is a powerful teacher, but it's a bear to go through. There was a long period of time where grief was a constant companion and it took its toll on me – both physically and emotionally. But it was years before I recognized this toll.

The years 2010 through 2015 were very difficult for me. In 2010, I began experiencing excruciating pain in my right hip. I did my best to ignore it and carry on. Living in denial wasn't difficult, at least not then. I learned to put up with the pain as time passed.

In 2010, my beloved canine, Magic, began showing his age. That year, after his fourteenth birthday, Magic's quality of life began to change. Always a healthy lad, health problems began to surface. He began to suffer from arthritis and he gradually developed dementia. When, one evening as he stood in our backyard in the pouring rain, confused, and couldn't figure out how to get back to the house, I wept. I finally understood what was happening to him.

I immediately put him on medication for both these ailments and, for a while, they helped. But Nature runs its course and there was only so much medication could do in the face of old age.

In late 2011, as Magic approached the age of sixteen, his body began to fail – his hearing and eyesight were failing and he became incontinent. As these ailments increased, I suffered too, with severe hip pain that I eventually learned was from a degenerating hip. I put myself into physical therapy, certain that this would "fix" things. Yet even with this care, my pain – both physical and emotional – from my dread at the inevitable decision I was facing - increased.

I grieved as my once proud, beautiful and independent Magic grew more feeble and I couldn't do anything to stop it. Going on walks became difficult. Walking over pavement without lines or seams, he hesitated more and more as if he couldn't figure out where to step. Letting him outside without supervision became risky. I always had to keep an eye on him to keep him safe.

As things progressed, I knew that I was facing one of the toughest decisions of my life. Many people in this position – with an elderly dog who's failing – would quickly more towards putting them down. But it was so very hard. He was my best friend and had been with me for so many years. I realized that our roles had changed – that he no longer was watching out for me but that I was now having to carefully watch every detail of his well-being like never before, to guard his safety.

The idea of ending Magic's life tore me apart and I was slow to come to that decision. It may sound selfish, but I knew that the day would come that I would have to show mercy, compassion and selflessness for my very best boy. I felt that as long as the medication could help keep him comfortable, I could love on him for just a while longer.

As the stress and upset about the looming decision about Magic grew, I seemed to physically deteriorate. I needed to use a cane all the time, to offset my stumbling painful walk. But nothing helped the almost unbearable pain in my heart. And once again, depression began creeping its way in.

After several months of heart wrenching soul-searching, I made the painful decision to put Magic to sleep. We had had 13 ½ wonderful, adventure-filled years together and, as he aged, I had prayed that I wouldn't have to face this terrible but necessary decision. But life said otherwise, while it continued to offer up other difficult and painful challenges as well.

Months before Magic passed, my Dad had become ill. As I

watched Magic decline, I also watched my Dad decline. Over the next few years, as he became physically and mentally weaker, I grieved for what was happening to him and for all that I and my family were losing. During much of this time period, I was also grieving deeply for Magic, and my grief increased the debilitating pain I was experiencing.

When the day in February 2012 finally came, I held a ceremony at my home to honor Magic and his passing. All the people who loved him were there, as was our vet and one of the monks from the nearby Buddhist monastery. Magic was loved on before he was put to sleep and bittersweet joy was present in the room as he slipped away. As that happened, my heart shattered.

Deep in grief and mourning for months for my lost companion, everything blended together. I was devastated. My mind was a blank. Nothing mattered. I stopped interacting with almost all of my friends. I didn't want to eat so I lost a lot of weight. I could hardly sleep and, when I did, I had vivid active dreams of Magic. I withdrew from all but the most basic "have to's". When I went to physical therapy, I would quietly weep through my exercises. Fortunately the staff had met Magic and they understood my grief.

I continued with physical therapy until I was finally forced to recognize that I wasn't healing and that I needed surgery to replace my now almost non-existent hip socket. The surgery, which took place in May 2012, went well and recovery plodded along. But my grief was still palpable.

That excruciating roller coaster ride of deep mourning lasted for almost a year. Along the way, various people tried to encourage and support me to move on more quickly, not understanding the level or intensity of my grief or my deep love and devotion for my dog.

"It's just a dog," they'd say. But they didn't know; didn't understand the bond we'd shared. Soulmates of different species is a real thing.

Eventually, I picked up the pieces of my life and began moving forward again. But to this day, years later, I still feel the ache of missing my best friend. The pain has lessened, as has the grief. And I have a new companion – my "class clown" Selby, who makes me laugh even when I don't want to. But the sadness, the longing for my beautiful Magic man, is still there, just below the surface, like an undercurrent ready to gently pull at my heart at a moment's notice.

Suffering the devastating loss of my friend and companion, I didn't recognize my symptoms of depression. Later, after I recognized the familiar deep pit I've been in, I once again began scaling up the walls of the rabbit hole, moving towards the light and an engaged and balanced life.

We can lose ourselves in that pit – sometimes for years. But what if we can catch a glimpse of the sun and remember who we are? When we do, we marvel at how we could have gotten so "lost". Remembering to take time to grieve and practice self-compassion are vital to recovering our spiritual and mental well-being, all of which impact our body and overall health This may be one of the toughest things we'll ever do, but making time to do these are what allows us to move forward to finding a healthy balance.

Okay, let's turn the tables a moment.

Looking at your life, what situations have taken place that have pushed you close to or over the edge? Can you pinpoint what happened to throw you into the depression pit? Taking the time to identify "what happened" is crucial. Write it down.

....

....

....

....

....

....

Now that you've identified the "what happened", how did it affect you? Did it result in illness of some sort? Did you hibernate or withdraw from friends, family, co-workers? Or something else? (With my "what happens". I would retreat, hibernating sometimes for months to lick my wounds until I felt safe enough to come back out again).

Be as specific as possible. It may reveal something significant to you.

Good for you. This is an important step. When we recognize what we're going through and give ourselves permission to go through it, we're finally able to move forward and climb out of the pit.

Take a look at what you just wrote. Think about what else you've learned from this. Is / are there any action(s) you might take the next time something related to this triggers your depression? Write it down here. And remember, be specific!

....

....

....

....

....

Good job. There are more insights still to come. So keep going!

Chapter 10

A Different View of Life: Choices Discovered

"Everything in your life is a reflection of a choice you
have made.

If you want a different result, make a different
choice."

—Anonymous

Life goes on and brings changes with it, whether we want
them to or not. And it's often been my experience that facing
big changes takes courage, although at those moments we may
not see it as that. Facing the loss of my dog, Magic, took more
courage than, at the time, I thought I had. Yet, as time passed, I
learned that I was stronger than I knew and could go on without
him at my side.

Choices

Depression has often seemed to be a thief, hiding in wait, biding
its time, ever ready to spring forth and rob me blind. It often
triggered unexpectedly but eventually, thankfully, I would come
out the other side, Still, I always knew that somewhere down the
road it would happen again. And again.

Yet I found there is a key – a tiny one – that can make a huge
difference when dealing with depression. No one talks about
this; at least I don't recall anyone specifically telling me about
this gem. If, perhaps, a former therapist did gift me with this
gold nugget, I am deeply grateful.

There are, as I said earlier, many types of depression and
everyone faces it differently But it's useful to know that just
maybe you might have a choice about how far down into the pit
you have to go.

The secret, this key, is deceptively simple. Mind you I didn't say
it's easy, merely that it's simple. And the key is this: There is
always a moment, perhaps a tiny, almost unnoticeable one,

when, if you really pay attention, you can choose to act or respond to that pendulum swing or crisis that's happening in your life. In my experience, depression is a response to something that happens – whether perceived or real - or something that's happening right now or happened in the past. You "become" depressed, going from one state to another.

This moment of choice and your ability to choose happens in an instant. It may whoosh softly through your mind, whispering, "Will you go down this familiar road again? Or will you have the courage to take a different, perhaps a less traveled, unfamiliar path?"

Too often over the years I've ignored or questioned that whisper and instead walked down a dark, rocky path. Yet those times I did recognize that moment, my choice led me onto a smoother, brighter road. I found this to be true in helping me deal with the loss of my beloved Magic as well as many other situations over the years.

So what does it take to recognize that moment? From what I can tell, it takes two things: willingness and awareness.

These two things – being willing and being aware of what's occurring - are wrapped around two important questions, the answers to which will determine and guide the direction you'll go. Ask yourself the following questions:

1. **Am I willing to accept that I can be the master of my own life and not be pushed around by life's circumstances? Can I accept that as a possibility?**

2. **Am I willing to hear that small voice when it softly announces itself and am I open to the possibility of listening to it when it does? Am I willing to make a commitment to do so?**

So what are your answers to the questions you've just read? Be honest with yourself. There's no right or wrong answer here.

Being willing to be the master of your life is a big step. You take that step forward by committing yourself to being willing. By doing that, you become responsible for yourself, your life, your reactions to circumstances. Being responsible isn't a dirty word. I believe your commitment to being responsible frees you. It frees you to stop blaming others for what happens to you. It lets you experience the power you have over your life. It lets you become the one driving the bus of your life.

But taking on being the master of your life doesn't mean you're shouldering a huge burden. True, sometimes thing can weigh on your shoulders. We all have those kind of days. But the larger picture here is your freedom to be.

I remember the first time that thought went through my head. It was in late 1978 – early 1979. I'd participated in a transformational program and was discovering LOTS of new ideas about how to live my life and how I wanted to be.

One day, I had an "ah-ha moment" where I suddenly realized that being responsible could be fun! Sounds crazy but true. In that moment I realized that I didn't have to keep blaming people for what was or wasn't happening in my life – not my parents, my siblings, my boss, no one. I could be responsible for what happened to me, which meant I could create what I wanted and how I wanted things to go. Sure, there would be circumstances and obstacles I'd have to overcome, but the bottom line was that I was ultimately going to be the pivotal, determining factor for me, not someone or something else.

This revelation was like fireworks going off! Suddenly I had buckets full of energy flying through me! Suddenly dreams were possible!

Plenty of people have had similar experiences – people who've gone from very difficult circumstances to rising above them to achieve success – people like Oprah Winfrey and Malala (Malala Yousafzai, the Pakistani activist who spoke up for education for girls). These people and so many others stepped forward in life, never letting their often severe, sometimes life-threatening circumstances get in their way of reaching their dreams, of making the biggest difference they could.

We see examples of this in movies too - like in "The Pursuit of Happyness," based on the real life of Chris Gardner.

Will Smith, who plays Gardner, becomes homeless and tries to sell medical equipment to make enough money to get back on his feet. At one point Gardner meets a man on the street, learns he's a stockbroker, and sees that as his path out of his desperate circumstances. Ultimately, Gardner joins Dean Witter Reynolds' training program, succeeds in it and moves forward to achieve extraordinary financial success.

Gardner had enormous faith, an ironclad belief that he could succeed and that he'd let nothing stop him. That faith and belief took him and his young son from homelessness to enormous success. Faith and hard work would lead him ultimately to open his own successful international holding company, become a successful motivational speaker and a well-respected philanthropist.

Being the master of your own life, driving your own bus, can be a terrifically exciting, rewarding path. Walking that path, knowing that depression can be around any corner, brings many challenges. But it is do-able.

I know. What you've just read may sound corny, simplistic, maybe even ridiculous. Maybe you'd have had a different reaction if you'd had that thought, that experience. BUT.. what if the underlying idea was true? WHAT IF you could be responsible, be the Master of your life? What if you didn't always have to react to things that triggered you and pushed you to fall into the depression pit – go down the rabbit hole? What if?

Whew! That's a lot to take in! Even acknowledging the possibility of this is a big deal; a big step. And don't think that once you do this, once you make the commitment to be willing, that your life will suddenly "turn out". It doesn't work that way. You'll still have ups and down. You'll have times you'll forget you even made that commitment! Sometimes you won't pay attention to that small voice whispering in your ear and you won't be willing to walk that not-always-familiar or comfortable path.

But then you'll remember again and you will pay attention. You'll re-commit yourself and things will begin to change.

Okay. Take a moment. Better yet, go back and reread the last few pages. When you consider this new possibility, how does all this make you feel?

Now write down your thoughts about what you've just read. What would be different if you were to become the master of your life? If you did indeed have a choice – even an occasional one - about whether or not to "become depressed." Even if the idea sounds completely far fetched, go ahead and use the space below to focus your thoughts and feelings about this. Consider the "what if" factor here. And, as always, BE SPECIFIC!

....

....

....

....

....

....

....

When we listen to that small voice, it allows us to step forward, not backward. If and when we hear and respond to that gentle nudge, we save ourselves so much anguish, so much lost time. The steps we take may be small, but by taking them we move forward and recognize the special gifts life offers us. Rather than having depression rob us blind from life's sweetness, by taking these steps, depression can eventually transform into "the blues." It can become less overwhelming, becoming something more manageable. This gives us the freedom to recover more quickly and to move forward more easily.

Freedom and choice - two important aspects of living a balanced fulfilling life. Let's look at a few more things that contribute to this.

Chapter 11

Living with Gratitude, Connecting & Being of Service

> "We might just give thanks for being alive, with the opportunity to contribute our best in this extraordinary time."

> *- Tony Seton, journalist, author, business/political consultant*

> "Gratitude is an art of painting an adversity into a lovely picture."

> --Kak Sri, November 2010 winner of the Quote Garden create your own quote contest on Twitter

We live in extraordinary times. But something's changed.

There used to be an undercurrent of hope and excitement in the air – of anticipation of what possibilities are around the corner.

Over the past few years, however, with the expansion of our communication networks and the growth of technology, we're more aware than ever of national and global crises and disasters. As our apprehension and anxiety levels rise, fear has tightened its grip on our collective psyche.

Many of us are stressed and worried beyond anything we've experienced before - especially over such a seemingly endless period. But in the midst of these incredibly trying times, we forget that we've been through other times where we've had big things to worry and be concerned about.

Remember the millennium debacle? For those who don't, a prediction surfaced that essentially said we'd suffer a world-wide catastrophic computer crash - resulting in planes falling out of the air and all sorts of mechanical disasters - at a specific date (which itself was in question). It didn't matter that this prophecy was made by the soothsayer Nostradamus[6] over 350 years

---

6   https://mudmap.wordpress.com/2012/07/01/flashback-nostrada-mus-and-y2k/</a><!--EndFragment-- !--EndFragment-->

before. Whether it was a credible prediction or not, companies and government agencies scrambled to find ways to safeguard critical data. For months, consumers suffered nightmares about the possible loss of their vital information and all kinds of technology failing completely – envisioning all sorts of catastrophes, including entire cities snarled to a standstill. Finally, after months filled with global anxiety and dread, when the clock struck midnight on December 31st, 1999 / January 1st, 2000, we discovered the much-feared disaster was a complete fizzle.

Many people bought into the anticipated Millennium disaster, though there was no concrete evidence it would happen. With visions of horrifying disaster playing out in the media and in everyone's imagination, many grabbed onto a terrifying fear of the unknown.

Fear can paralyze us – if we let it. But there's always the other side of the coin to consider: what if? What if that terrible thing you fear doesn't happen? What if a terrific opportunity shows up instead? What if you imagine THAT rather than the worst that could occur?

If we take the time and make the effort, we can see plenty of what I consider to be miracles in our lives. They come in all shapes, sizes and varieties. Sure, there's always the huge, life-altering kind. But what I'm talking about are the less dramatic ones. Things like having a home you love, good friends you get to spend time with, a dog or cat who idolizes you or even a simple sunlit day. THOSE are just as much miracles as the HUGE ones we read about, don't you think?

Grumbling about what's missing in our lives is easy. But what if you took a step back and looked at the bigger picture? What do you have to be grateful for? That's something I often forget to do. I get caught up in circumstances and in dealing with "stuff" and worrying about what's happening around me and in the world. Pretty soon, I'm a bundle of worry and my life starts to get pretty gloomy. And, if I'm not careful, that depression pit will seductively beckon once more.

But let's tell the truth here. Does doing this – worrying til we're practically ill, panicking over things gone wrong – does it enhance the quality of our lives? Does it make us feel better, more energized, more joyful? I'd bet the answer to these questions is a resounding "no!" If that's so, then what? Clearly there's got to be another choice we can make that will enliven us more, bring more sunlight and ease and laughter to our lives.

Life is a gift, and how we use it is up to us.

Making gratefulness a part of our daily routine is an important element that helps us lead a life of balance and fulfillment. Let's look at what you're grateful for. We all have something we can point to. Write down at least 3 things for which you are grateful in the space below.

....

....

....

....

....

....

You may want to keep this list handy and read through it regularly. Update it as you find more things you're grateful for. Doing this can be part of putting into place your gratefulness routine. And I suspect you'll find that practicing this regularly helps keep you on a more even, balanced keel.

Connecting

To be able to let go of how we've always reacted and/or thought of things requires a shift in perspective. In a world where being in touch is just a finger tap away, our connections are what lift us up and help us view things differently.

Connecting with others – not only online on social media but really connecting and sharing yourself - seeing a need and taking action to address it, contributing our time and energy towards solving a problem – these are the actions that touch peoples lives in a positive, uplifting way. And the impact of our willingness to reach out and touch people's lives can be profound.

Think back for a moment. Have you ever had a stranger stop and gave you a compliment out of the blue? Chances are it made you feel good. I make it a habit to compliment people when I'm out and about. If I see someone who looks great or is wearing something bright or something striking, I stop and compliment them. It always brings a smile to their face. My small gesture makes someone's day a little better.

Like many of us, I've gone through some rough times. I was fortunate in that many people "helped" me through them. What I've learned from this is the more you allow others to be of service, the more you serve them too. Giving to other people takes our attention off ourselves and turns the spotlight on someone else. Serving others brings out the finest in us. True, we give our best during emergencies, or when we don't have time to think, just react. But consider this – when did you last give more of yourself than what you believed you could? Did you surprise yourself when you did?

A former radio personality I know always ended his show by encouraging listeners to "take time and do a random act of kindness." Being of Service – as part of a group or one-on-one – is a special way we touch people's lives.

Giving of yourself, being of service to someone, has an added benefit. Placing your attention on someone else helps you sidestep depression and its triggers. And doing so will likely spark feelings of contentment and happiness. These feelings just aren't possible alongside depression.

So maybe doing random acts of kindness is one important action step that can help us get out of depression. It's worth trying, wouldn't you say?Here's a question. Are there some actions you could take that would allow you to be of service to someone (or something)? Think about those random acts of kindness I mentioned earlier. List two or three steps or actions you could take below.

....

....

....

....

....

....

....

Now let's turn these action steps into something more concrete. After all, this is about not being depression's victim and to be able to go that direction takes action. So answer this. What will it take for you to get into action? And by when will you take that action? Is there something that must happen first before you can take action – some other step you have to take? Write it down below. Then write the "by when" you'll take that next step. And, as always, please be specific!

....

....

....

....

....

....

Okay. Are you starting to get a glimmer of where this is going? Can you begin to see the brush strokes of the larger picture here?

These exercises you've been doing have a purpose. Each successive one has been building on the one before. They're part of a conscious design - a Strategy for Success. [7]This often business-related planning tool is one you can tailor to your personal needs and use when you find you're heading towards depression.

Designing and customizing this Plan is a significant step on your path to not letting depression make you its victim. As you work through the exercises in this book, you're developing a powerful tool kit packed with new positive actions. This tool kit can be your "go-to" the next time depression rears its head.

So read on. Let's expand on what you've just completed and examine other possibilities.

---

7   "Five Essentials of an Effective Strategy", Mark Rhodes; June 7, 2010. https://managementhelp.org/blogs/strategic-planing/2010 /06/07/five-essentials-of-an-effective-strategy/

Chapter 12

What Happens When ... Questions to Dive Into

"It takes courage to grow up and turn out to be who you really are."

– e.e. cummings

Let's face it. Depression stinks.

All kinds of circumstances can trigger depression. It can be as simple as an argument with your best friend or that raise or bonus you expected that doesn't materialize. Or finding out that a project you've completed had something left out or it contained mistakes and your boss is furious. Depression can happen when you've quarreled with a family member who wrongly accuses you of something or when something mundane happens like discovering your washing machine sprung a leak and you don't have the money to fix it.

Questions to Dive In To

What happens when you fall into depression?

We pay a price when we fall into depression. It can stop us in our tracks. We stop working or just go through the motions; we quit seeing friends and loved ones; we stop going out to do anything fun. We eat only enough to survive or we pig out on anything we can get out hands on for comfort.

When I've been deep in depression, I "hibernate" - stewing in a solitude filled with anguish and pain. I've done it for days, even weeks. I've literally spent days just staring into space for who knows how long or just stared out the window. During those times, nothing made sense to me and I couldn't get myself to move or do anything. All I could do was suffer and hunker down into that pit.

But I've been very, very lucky to have friends who know me and who aren't willing to let me stew forever. Sometimes, a brave soul has shown up at my door and insisted I get out and do ordinary things like grocery shopping or go for a walk (since I clearly wouldn't do it by or for myself at that point.

I remember the first time a good friend showed up at my house after I'd been "hibernating" for several weeks. He knew I was home and kept knocking and calling out to me until I was annoyed enough to finally answer the door. I was pretty nasty to him and tried my best to get him to leave me alone. Fortunately, he wouldn't take no for an answer and cajoled me into coming out with him on some simple errands. He gently pulled me along to be out with people, getting me slowly used to being back out in the world again. In the end, I was really grateful to him – and very impressed with his courage!

When we eventually drag ourselves out of the depression pit, it's shocking to discover how deep down we've gone. I've been astonished time and again that I wasn't able to see things that had been right in front of me – simple choices I could have made or actions I could have taken to help myself move forward. Because of the deep pit I'd been in, I had tunnel vision and only saw walls so high I couldn't see above or around them.

My depression has affected every aspect of my life. It's blinded me and monochromed my actions, responses, emotions, relationships and my career. I've rarely talked about or mentioned it to friends. Over the past few years when I finally began opening up and talking about it, my friends were stunned. I'd been so skillful in hiding or masking what was going on that they had no clue.

Depression has been ever-present in my life. It took me years to gain important tools that helped me see that I had a choice; that there were indeed steps / actions I could take to help myself.

How do you step away from the abyss?

Depression isn't pretty or funny or entertaining. It hurts – inside and all around. It steals your ability to think clearly and, at its worst, to function. Bottom line – it robs you blind.

If there's one thing I've learned over the years, it's that courage is fundamental in helping to pull back from the brink when every impulse screams at you to walk down that dark familiar path.

To step out of what's comfortable and say to depression "No, not today. You won't get me," is perhaps the most powerful, courageous action you'll ever take. Today (and every day), if we want to create something different - a fresh approach, a better way of living life - we must make different choices, and continue making them, sometimes many times a day. The old saying is still true: "If you do what you've always done, you'll get what you always got." It's never a one and done deal.

What can you do to help yourself?

It takes effort to stay out of depression. Sure, sometimes it's doing simple things like getting up from the chair or the couch and moving. For me, dancing around the living room is a great depression buster. Did you know it's almost impossible to stay sad or depressed when you're dancing to upbeat music? Try it now and see for yourself. Make sure the music is UPBEAT when you do this. Then come back to the book!

How did dancing make you feel? List three emotions in the space below that you felt while you were dancing. And, as always, be specific.

....

....

....

....

....

Moving – and dancing – are just a couple of techniques you can use to help you sidestep depression. Are there other simple actions you can think of that would help you as well? List at least two of them below.

....

....

....

....

....

....

Depression effects everyone differently and we each deal with it differently. Those who face this darkness know that during troubled times, reaching out to friends or family – as hard as it may be - is a great first step. But when things get rough, when circumstances feel unbearable or overwhelming, that's when it takes more than having a sympathetic shoulder to lean on. That's when seeing a professional could be your best next step. Their job is to guide us through a path strewn with challenges and big boulders. By helping present the bigger picture versus our personal tunnel vision, they help us gain a wider, more empowering perspective and they offer techniques we can use to help us get past our obstacles.

Chapter 13

Miracles, Challenges and Loss Equals More Choice

Hope is realizing you are bigger than your past.

--- Anonymous

"All life is an experiment. The more experiments you make, the better."

- Ralph Waldo Emerson

Life can surprise you. Remember back in the introduction I said I view life as a tapestry? Well, so often, there are unexpected, unexplainable instances or circumstances that added a richness to the tapestry's fabric and to the quality of our lives. I call those everyday miracles. Sometimes they're as simple as someone you really wanted to talk to calls you out of the blue. Or maybe you're having a tough time doing something and someone unexpectedly reaches out to help. Maybe you phoned someone thinking you needed moral support only to discover that person was having a tough time and you could be there for them instead.

I'll bet if you think about it, you'll find a lot of similar circumstances have happened in your life. Lots of these everyday miracles have woven through the tapestry of my life – both large and small. But, undoubtedly, the most incredible of these were, for me, the three times I've become depression free. As I mentioned in Chapter 1, during these extraordinary times life looked brighter; my energy seemed limitless; I laughed freely and problems became much more manageable.

But change is a constant in life. When the first two "depression free" times suddenly ended, I was devastated. But having experienced what living without depression could be like, I realized I'd been given a gift. I'd learned what an unfettered, unburdened, open and joyful life really could be. The idea that I could live this way changed my perspective about what was possible.

Remarkably, in 2018, I found myself depression free for a third time. This time, though, it occurred during one of the most challenging times of my life.

In late May 2018, I had my second hip replacement surgery. For two weeks afterwords, I lived with pain and a constant regimen of antibiotics and pain meds. At my post surgery two week follow-up appointment, I peppered my surgeon with questions, including how soon I could stop taking the narcotic he'd prescribed for pain, which I was eager to be off of. The doctor said I could now take it "as needed" and that I could immediately begin taking an over-the-counter pain reliever instead.

Later that evening when I searched my go-to bag at home, I pulled out what I thought was my ibuprofen. Instead I discovered it was my bottle of antidepressants! Having taken them like clockwork every day for years, I somehow had forgotten to take them for two whole weeks! I was shocked!

Let me be clear here. NO ONE SHOULD TRY THIS! I would NEVER knowingly have done this. The chance of getting into serious trouble, of falling into a real and serious health crisis by taking this kind of risk, is HUGE. You do not play with fire.

Clearly this was an extraordinary situation. What was I supposed to do now? Should I start taking the meds again and, if so, at what level? Or should I keep doing what I'd been doing, which was do without them? After all, as my pain from the surgery steadily decreased, I found I was happier, I was sleeping well and was otherwise in good spirits. With no clue as to what action to take, I called a good friend, a nurse with decades of emergency room experience, for advice. After much discussion, we agreed that since I was doing fine, I should continue without adding my antidepressants back and that I should monitor my progress as I went forward. Amazingly, years later, all continues to be well.

Challenges and Loss Can Equal More Choice

I mentioned earlier that for years my relationship with my parents had been difficult. The last few years of their lives – between 2010 and 2018 - we were able to resolve most of the issues between us. This enabled me to make one of the biggest, most important choices of my life.

As my relationship with my parents got better, we were more at ease with each other; we listened better, argued less and enjoyed our time together in a way we hadn't for decades. Wanting to spend more time with them, I began traveling more frequently from California to South Texas to visit. With each visit, I had hopes that we could shift our relationships from parent-child more towards being close friends. I'd seen this with some of my friends and their parents and longed to have this with my own.

But this wasn't meant to be. Cruel circumstances would rob us of that opportunity.

My Dad developed Alzheimer's the last several years of his life. This wicked disease was the worst kind of master thief. With my heart breaking. I watched this man who had been such a leader in the community, who had been so sharp intellectually and so strong minded, become unsure, forgetful and frail. It was so terribly unfair! And there was nothing anyone could do to stop it or slow it down.

I felt very fortunate, though. Whenever I came into town, Dad always seemed to know who I was – perhaps not remembering my name but always that I was his daughter. A big smile would light up his face each time he'd first see me. During each visit, there were often very small magical moments where he'd suddenly be "there", be fully himself. These times were so fleeting, yet were times I came to treasure for those precious glimpses of seeing my Dad again.

While my Dad was steadily declining mentally into Alzheimer's, my Mom was slowing down as well. Dad's steadily failing health clearly wore on her. To be closer to my Dad, she cut back almost completely going out with friends. She almost always stayed home with Dad or, whenever he was in the hospital, spent hours sitting at his bedside. This vital, active woman slowly and steadily slipped into a sedentary lonely lifestyle. Try as I might to suggest she go out to lunch with friends or attend some event, she almost always said no. And as time went on and she did less and less, I worried for her health and her mental well being.

Knowing that being active and engaged are vital to retaining mental clarity, I rightly feared she would go down the same path my Dad was on. It was achingly sad to watch.

As I said back in Chapter 6, even during our toughest, darkest moments we have the opportunity to make a conscious choice in the face of depression. Although that moment of choice may be fleeting, IT'S THERE. Ignore or refuse it and the darkness takes over. Recognize and step forward into that Choice and new possibilities present themselves. Actively making a choice and choosing a direction is the critical factor to discovering the real juice and joy of life.

After several years of steadily declining health, my father died in October 2015. As sad as I was at this terrible loss, I was grateful for all the time we'd had together. We had almost lost my Dad a number of times the lasts few years of his life. Yet he'd always been brought back to life. As proud a man as he was, it was excruciating to see him come back to a life where he grew increasingly unable to remember things and his loved ones and one where he was a shell of his former self. I know that the end was a release and relief to his spirit. I still miss him terribly and often wish for just a few more minutes to speak with him again. But I have no regrets. We were so lucky to have the time we had together.

Months after my father's death, during the spring of 2016 – knowing the upheaval it would require of me, knowing how much of what I loved and treasured about my surroundings and lifestyle that I would be giving up - I voluntarily uprooted myself from my beloved Northern California and moved back to Texas. Because Mom and I had resolved so much between us, it was a natural choice for me to make.

Losing my Dad made me appreciate being with my Mom even more. I hoped we would have many years together. But once again, my expectations led to keen disappointment and sadness. As John Lennon said, "life is what happens to you when you're busy making other plans."

In late May, 2018, I had my second hip replacement. Three

weeks later, my Mother had a stroke. For weeks she was in intensive care, drifting in and out of a coma. When she was awake, we shared music, stories about old friends and she sometimes even cracked a joke. Unfortunately after that first week, she became unable to talk. But we still had cause for hope. When she was awake, which happened frequently, she was very alert and responsive. These times were definitely small miracles – we were told that coming out of a coma periodically the way she did rarely happens.

Sadly Mom slipped back fully into the coma the third week, apparently for good this time, and her doctors in the Intensive Care Unit (ICU) told us there was nothing else they could do for her. So we brought her home, ostensibly to die. Only she clearly had other ideas!

My Mom was with us for another remarkable three weeks, again slipping in and out of consciousness. Her awake times ranged from ten to thirty minutes at a time. Although unable to speak, when awake she nevertheless was alert and tracked what was said.

During those weeks, I had moved into my Mother's house to be near her. Even though she had caregivers, we spent many hours of those days and nights together. While she "slept," I would play her favorite music; talk to her; hold her hand. When she was awake, I'd try to make her laugh. And I'd grab the phone, reaching out to my nephews, my brother or sisters to have them talk with Mom. Each time I'd hold the phone to her ear and as they spoke with her, I'd watch her face light up. I saw her really listen and really focus. Did she understand what was said to her or who was talking? Who knows. But these times gave everyone the chance to connect with Mom and, perhaps, for her to feel connected with them.

As the weeks passed, we all held onto hope that Mom would somehow recover or at least get a little better. Sadly there was no hope to be had. Twice it seemed Mom was transitioning into passing away. I stayed by her side each night these times happened, holding her hand, telling her it was alright to let go. And each time, the next morning, amazingly, she'd still be there, unconscious but still alive. It was as if she kept deciding it 87 wasn't the right time to go yet.

As I said, my Mother was a force of Nature - strong willed, stubborn but fair and she did things the way she felt was best. And that's how she did things all the way through to the end.

And the end did inevitably arrive. After three weeks of being in and out of consciousness, my Mom passed peacefully away in early August, 2018.

During the last three years of her life, Mom and I became close. Although we didn't live together, we saw each other every few days and had daily phone conversations. Weekends were our special time. We'd go out for lunch, go see old movies or just hang out and talk or watch tv. Knowing how important it was for her to get out and be with people in public, to enjoy herself, and knowing she wouldn't go out on her own, I arranged for us to go to the local performing arts theater to enjoy musical performances by Broadway touring groups or famous musicians of her era like Tony Bennett. We'd also go out to brunch and dinner regularly. Old friends were thrilled to see her and she them.

Occasionally I would fix a yummy gourmet vegetarian dinner for her at her home, sometimes inviting one of her friends to join us. We'd linger at the dinner table, laughing, talking and sharing stories. Mom had a wicked sense of humor and I worked hard to stay sharp just to keep up with her! These bright spots in my Mom's last years brought her joy and brought me the pleasure of her company and, most importantly, of making a difference in the quality of her life.

After Mom passed, I was stunned to realize I was now an orphan. True, I was well into my 60's and all my siblings were alive and in good health. But losing my second parent put me adrift. Whenever I would drive through my former hometown or go by what had been my parents house, it felt foreign. I felt I didn't belong anywhere. Without my Mom, my anchor was gone. There was no more "Atlas hacienda" (my house in a nearby small town didn't count). For the first time in decades, there was no Atlas elder in the town where they'd lived, raised a family, been civic leaders and been cherished friends to so many for over 60 years.

For me, during this time I felt as if I was sailing a small ship with no rudder and no clear sight of the shore.

Life is full of triggers – things that happen that can suddenly lead you towards depression. Losing both of my parents could understandably could have been triggers that could have led me into a deep depression. Somehow, miraculously, it didn't.

But let's turn it back to you for a moment. What situations or circumstances in your life have triggered you, pushed you up to or over the edge? Did someone say something hurtful or that you felt was unjust? Did an action someone took upset you? It might have seemed to be a small thing but those are often the kinds of things that have triggered me.

Take a moment and write down at least three of these situations that triggered you towards depression. Not the story but the specific actions – the "what happened", be it was spoken, written or implied – that were the triggers for you falling down the rabbit hole.

....

....

....

....

....

....

Now look through what you just wrote. Consider some alternative possibilities. What would have helped you step back from your rabbit hole in these situations if you'd had something or someone to support you, to reach out to? And what would you want to have in place to help yourself the next time you get triggered and find yourself standing on the edge of your personal abyss?

Do you already have a support system you can tap into when and if that happens?

If not, who or what is missing? And what can you begin to do to set that up?

What are some ideas and action steps you can take to create a strong support net for yourself? Be aware that doing this may be outside your comfort zone. Remember, no man is an island. No one of us truly makes it to success all by themselves in this world.

There's no time like now, dear reader. Who could you reach out to to ask to be part of your support team? Maybe it's a friend, a colleague you really like, maybe a relative. You can start putting together a solid, count-on-able team, people you can rely on to be there for you when you need them.

Time to get writing! Think of those support possibilities! The more you add, the more likely things will start moving forward. And be specific here!

....

....

....

....

....

....

You'll want to set up a conversation with the people on your list, to let them know you'd like their support and ask them to be part of your team. Asking for support helps build connections and creates a safety net you can count on to help you stay back from that rabbit hole. Remember, by asking others for help when things get tough you're setting yourself up to succeed the next time depression pushes you to the edge.

Taking these steps is another part of creating your Strategy for Success. A key element to success is setting goals and taking steps to achieve them. So, here's another important question. By when will you take the actions you've just thought of? Go back through what you've just written and put a specific time frame, a "by when" next to your intended actions. Remember, you've done this before so this time should be easier. Putting a time frame to your intended action helps you stay on track and establish a strong, reliable, empowering support system. It's one of the key elements that has you win at being able to step away from the abyss of depression.

Chapter 14

Different Directions Bring Surprises and Changing Your Conversation

"A mind that is stretched to a new idea never returns to its original dimensions."

—Albert Einstein / Oliver Wendall Holmes

"For every thing you have missed, you have gained something else; and for every thing you gain, you lose something else. "

—Ralph Waldo Emerson (1803 - 1882)

For three months after my Mother died and the aching loss of her became the new normal, Mom's housekeeper Anna and I went through Mom's house and her vast array of treasured things. Everywhere I looked and everything I touched reminded me she was gone. The work of going through Mom's cabinets, drawers and closets was often heart-wrenching. Daily I longed to have at least one, if not both, of my sisters there to help and to share the experience and memories with me. Tears would often well up throughout Anna's and my efforts. At the end of each day I'd go home exhausted and spent.

Yet sifting through the countless pictures, momemtoes and just plain stuff Mom had collected allowed me to relive wonderful yet long-forgotten memories. For example, I spent an entire day going through three large boxes filled with file folders and notebooks of recipes, and spent a half day going through her many, many cookbooks. As I did, I remembered when Mom taught herself to be a gourmet cook. I must have been around ten or eleven years old. The more proficient Mom became, the higher quality food she served. I remembered the scrumptious desserts she used to make – her yummy pineapple upside down cake, her scrumptious blueberry coffeecake and her famous lemon bars. Strolling down memory lane I recalled her story of how she learned how to cook "Jewish food" from Grandma

(Dad's mother), a wonderful cook who never used a recipe.

I remembered Mom telling me how she'd spent an afternoon just sitting and observing Grandma as prepared her sweet and sour cabbage, taking careful notes and asking endless questions so that she could get as close to Grandma's "recipe" as possible. And she definitely did a great job as I and the rest of my family were the happy beneficiary of Mom's superb Jewish cooking.

So many memories washed over me during these difficult times. For example, as I've said before, Mom was a Presence, a force of Nature. You knew to be on your best behavior around her – or else! Parents in town knew this about Mom. In our small town back then, parents acted as surrogate parents to their kids friends so kids knew they'd be disciplined for bad behavior. And Mom was a stickler for good behavior and good manners! Even as adults, one of the "kids" I grew up with told me how terrified she'd been by being around Mom's mojo during the last year of Mom's life. She kept that skill to the very end.

There were so many memories to process and to treasure. My brother Scott, who lived out of town, would come in some weekends and we would go through thousands of photographs and more than 60 photo albums together. Memories flooded us both. Sifting through photographs of people we'd grown up with – old friends and sometimes relatives long gone – often made us laugh, recalling fun times we had shared with them or trips we'd all taken.

For my part, I could only go through these a few hours at a time. More than that was too much for me to handle. Thankfully, he stayed the course, working into the evening each time he was in town. I really appreciated his dedication and hard work. I know it must have taken a toll on him as well although he never showed it.

Eventually we got through it all.

As I've said, life is full of surprises. One of them was that throughout this emotional turmoil – the grief and the tsunami of memories crashing over me, never once did I stand at the edge of the abyss or fall into depression. I definitely experienced deep sadness and I felt the loss of my Mom terribly. Yet only once through all that time period did I even flirt with the idea of depression. At that moment, I used the skills I'd gained over the years – skills like moving, dancing around, reaching out to others for support - to sidestep it and find my balance again.For months I'd been immersed in emotion-triggering circumstances, but because I'd stayed fairly centered, I began to understand the distinctions between being sad, having "the blues", and being depressed. Vigilantly I watched for any signs of depression but thankfully saw none.

Still, today, I keep my fingers crossed things will stay this way. But only time will tell. Meanwhile, my life – with its ups and downs, with circumstances and the chaos and uncertainty that life brings – stays fairly balanced.

In telling my story, I realize that I often jump around in time. But this method allows me to focus on and build the story to its high point. So I hope you'll bear with me as I slide down that path yet again.

Throughout my adult life I've had some remarkable experiences, many of which have been like talisman or touchstones I've used in times of difficulty to help me find my balance again. One such experience gave me insights I use to this day to help me step back from the depression pit. Perhaps this story can be useful to you, too.

Back in Chapter 1, I mentioned that I'd had Chronic Fatigue in the Fall of 1996. Recovery and healing seemed to take a long time. In early 1997, a friend and colleague planned to lead a retreat in Maui and he invited me to attend. As my strength and stamina were building, I decided to go. It would be my first major excursion since being so ill and my first time ever in Hawaii, so I was really excited!

The island of Maui was beautiful – with its clean windswept beaches, its colorful, exotic birds and wildlife. Each morning, birdsong would waft magically through the air as I walked from the sleeping cabins to the main house to help prepare breakfast and then attend the workshop sessions. The week-long retreat was everything I'd hoped it would be.

Although our retreat schedule was very full, during some of our rare "time off", a group of us decided to seize the moment to drive upcountry to Haleakala, the dormant volcano that forms over 75 percent of the island of Maui. As the altitude increased, what had begun as a warm, partly cloudy day morphed into a gloomy, dark afternoon of steady drizzle. After parking in the Haleakala Park parking lot, everyone went in multiple directions, eagerly exploring the trails that looped around and down into the caldera. I, however, stayed up top, meditating, marveling at the panoramic view as an amazing weather display unfolded before me. Gigantic white clouds of all shapes and sizes rose and billowed, filling the sky. They quickly transformed into cloud palaces, shapes reminiscent of wild creatures and fantastical designs. As swiftly as these phantoms appeared, however, gentle winds blew them away, replacing them with others. This exquisite pattern repeated again and again.

Watching this natural spectacle, I was awestruck by this dramatic and beautiful display. I realized I was viewing one of Nature's miracles. Although I was seeing a seemingly gray, drizzly sky, just above that was an azure blue, sunshine-filled sky. As I sat astonished at the ever changing majesty of these clouds, people down-country only saw the black storm clouds rolling steadily across the gray sky above them. They never knew about the brilliantly beautiful blue sky above them.

Suddenly, it was as if a lightning bolt struck me. What we see and our reaction to it is all about our perspective. Put simply: there can be blue skies above yet gray clouds below that obscure that beauty Or consider this: if you knew for sure there was a gorgeous blue sky above the rotten weather you were experiencing, would it change how you felt, what you thought, how you experienced things? Definitely something to think about.

This thought has come back to me many times as I've struggled through challenging times. It's easy to forget that the clouds we see (or experience as difficult circumstances in our lives) look different depending on where we stand (i.e. our perspective). When you live with depression, it's easy to find ourselves on the gloomy side of the cloud, unaware of the beautiful blue   95 skies above. If you can somehow peek through that gloom or even just remember it's there, the blue sky above may pull you upward into that grand expanse.

As the years have passed, and as I often reflect on my experience at Haleakala, I've continued to learn that our perceptions change and, as a result, so do our perspectives. Here's an example from my life.

In 1997, I became a Buddhist. I'd always been a seeker but I'd never imagined I'd actually convert. Having been raised Jewish, converting was a very big deal. Yet when I discovered Buddhism and visited a Buddhist monastery for the first time, it felt like coming home.

I've found over the years that my Buddhist practice has served me in many ways. Practicing the "Middle Way" - always seeking that other option besides the obvious left hand or right hand choices – has helped provide balance in my life.

For most of my life, my depression had often masked a deep anger that I'd held just under the surface – anger at how, growing up, I felt so different from everyone else, anger at how people treated (or mistreated) others. I rarely had a good outlet to express that anger so, like my depression, I kept it bottled up inside. And like many geysers, my anger would sometimes bubble up and explode.

After embracing Buddhism and its practices, my anger began to cool and my ability to relate to and with others increased. This showed in my relationships with my parents, as I've already mentioned, as well as with friends and with my siblings.

Not long ago, a family member and I had a discussion that escalated beyond differing opinions. During our conversation, our dissimilar values and vastly different perspectives collided, leaving both of us angry and upset. They accused me of doing something I hadn't and, taking it personally, I found myself on the edge of depression. The swirling tangle of emotions threatened overwhelm me and to drag me down. Struggling for balance and stability, I was able to step back from the situation and see that it wasn't a personal attack. It was instead a clash of values and perspective. Seeing this, I was finally able to sidestep my anger and frustration and calm down. From that vantage point, I went back to my sibling and, during that second conversation, we were able to peacefully resolve our issues.

Sometime later, I recalled that years before, my Mother and I had had similarly heated conversations about choices I'd made that she disagreed with – decisions like my plan to move across the country and my decision to change careers. Our conversations were predictable – each of us with different points of view, unwilling to listen to the other. Mom would list the negative things associated with my choices and I'd get angry. We'd both end up frustrated; the conversation would stall, tempers would flare and the "discussion" would devolve into a contest of wills with no winner.

After becoming a Buddhist, my perspective seemed to change. I began to realize that what I perceived as my Mom's negativity was in fact her upside-down way of telling me she loved me. Realizing this helped take the charge off of my perception of what she was saying and I eased back from my automatic argumentative response.

The next time a similar conversation happened, things went differently. Instead of arguing or getting angry, I simply said "I love you too, Mom." She would get flustered, her negative diatribe stopped and our conversations moved on. There definitely began to be more peace between us.

Looking at these perception filters - that which allows us to perceive or draw conclusions about what someone says or does - brings to mind something called <u>Neuro-Linguistic Programmiing</u> (NLP) . Within that system is a technique called reframing [8] At its simplest, reframing is taking something that you've perceived was done or said and turning it around so that you see it from a different perspective, in another light, an alternate, generally more positive point of view.

Doing this as a conscious deliberate choice helps us see things differently. It changes our perspectives and our behavior.

Consider how I shifted my reaction and response to my Mom. I changed how I perceived what she told me. I reframed it so that I altered my attitude about it. By doing this, what I perceived as negative became something positive, even empowering. By altering what an experience means to you, you can change your response to it.

Although I have never studied NLP, I've been fortunate to have friends who were NLP practitioners or who have embraced NLP and they shared some of its techniques with me.. Knowing this reframing technique has helped me recognize that changing my perception, my internal conversation about something negative, is vital. It's a step towards reclaiming personal power. The more I practice this technique, the more likely I will stay away from the edge of depression. It's another powerful strategy that helps me stay balanced amidst circumstances.

Thinking back on the conflict with my family member – when I was accused of purposefully doing something that reflected badly on their reputation when I hadn't done anything - I began to see it in a different perspective. Instead of feeling angry and frustrated or wanting to lash out at being unjustly accused, I stepped back, reframed my perspective, and realized they were trying to tell me something. Behind the accusation was a desire to have me on their side, to be their ally, not a combatant. This was not only a new thought for me, particularly in this situation, this realization also helped me step away from both my anger and from the possibility of falling into depression.

I hope these examples and stories have been useful so far. Now the ball's in your court. Are there situations you react to emotionally that might have another side, a different message to give you? If you step back from a situation or incident that happened and take another look, like the examples you just read where family members said hurtful, negative statements and then I reframed what had happened and discovered what they were actually trying to say - what situations in your life might be comparable?

Write at least 3 of these situations here. First, list (briefly) what happened, then try reframing the situation by identifying what a positive underlying message might actually be. Look and reframe beyond the "what happened" - try to get underneath it and see what else was going on. And be specific!

What Was Said	What Was Meant

....
....
....
....
....
....
....
....

I know this exercise wasn't easy. But thanks for being willing to do it! What you've written reveals a lot – and can be useful as you go forward, as you continue to build your strategy for stepping back from depression.

Our internal conversation – our perspective – affects everything we do. To thrive as someone who lives with depression, it's critical to have support and to gain important skills to help yourself, such as the NLP technique I mentioned. But, as the vast number of books and articles available on the subject show, there are a variety of different opinions and methods to address depression. No one method is "the" answer for everyone. The key is to identify what works for you and then embrace it.

Like any life journey, no one gets through depression alone and thrives. Working with a qualified health professional as part of your Wellness Team may be your key to achieving emotional balance. It certainly has been in mine.

Adding an experienced therapist, psychotherapist or trained counselor to your Wellness Team means having invaluable support and someone who will hold the "bigger picture" for you. Remember the analogy earlier of that blue sky above the dark gloomy clouds? As I've found so many times, you may discover that your own perspective may not be an empowering one. A trained support person can help you become aware of possibilities you might not have been able to see. Cognitive therapy [9]is a type of talk therapy that I've participated successfully in. It emphasizes the substitution of desirable patterns of thinking for manipulative or faulty ones. [10]This relatively short-term therapy focuses on how you think, behave and communicate rather than on early childhood experiences. [11]And that's another vital tool to helping you step away from the edge.

You'll want to take time to search until you you identify someone you feel comfortable working with, then commit to doing the work for as long it takes.

Don't set an arbitrary 'by when' to be complete. That will limit you and you may miss out on some vital work that could make a big difference for you. By working with that support person, you'll learn important skills to help you spot depression before it grabs you, as well as actions you can take to sidestep or minimize its effect. All this will serve you well over time.

Having these skills has made a tremendous difference in my life. They have helped me keep getting up when life knocks me down, and I can honestly say that even with depression, it's possible to live a life that's engaging, exciting, creative and, yes, fun! It comes down to the choices you make, the actions you take, the support you create for yourself and the internal conversations you have about it all.

---

9   https://www.merriam-webster.com/dictionary/cognitive%20therapy

10   https://www.merriam-webster.com/dictionary/cognitive%20therapy

11   https://www.cognitivetherapynyc.com/What-Is-Cognitive-Therapy.aspx

Chapter 15

Not an Ending - an Empowering Beginning

"May Light always surround you; Hope kindle
and rebound you. May your Hurts turn to Healing;
Your Heart embrace Feeling. May Wounds become
Wisdom; Every Kindness a Prism. May Laughter
infect you; Your Passion resurrect you. May
Goodness inspireyour Deepest Desires. Through all
that you Reach For,May your arms Never Tire."

-D. Simone

Inspiration has always been an important factor in my life. Being inspired not only motivates me, it also lifts me up. As someone who lives with depression, I find that seeking and discovering inspiration on a regular basis is one key way I use to stay balanced, particularly when the environment around me is difficult or distressing.

Throughout my life, a number of people have inspired me. Not surprisingly, one of them was Fred Rogers, TV's Mister Rogers. He always shared such simple yet profound wisdom. Paraphrasing him, often when you think you're at the end of something, you discover you're at the beginning of something else.[12]

When you come to the end of the road – such as a career gone sideways, an ending of a relationship, any chapter in your life that's come to an end - aren't you then at the beginning of another path? This is definitely a case of reframing and certainly a more positive perspective, don't you think?

---

12   From The World According to Mister Rogers: Important Things to Remember by Fred Rogers; Hachette Books (October 8, 2003).

My hope for all of us is that our lives will be filled with feelings that come from deep caring - delight, sadness, joy, wisdom - and that in all the endings we experience in our lives, we will recognize the new beginnings right in front of us.

Writing a book is a long, often tedious process. First you have to figure out a strong beginning (figuring out beginnings and endings has always been tough for me). Then you slog through the chronology, the details and memories of what took place, then work hard to make sense of it. Most important of all, you need to discover how to engage your readers so they'll want to keep reading, especially when the subject matter is a tough one like depression.

During the more than twelve years it took me to write this book, recalling the painful memories would periodically toss me over the edge into my dark pit. When I'd drag myself out, I would realize what a pivotal time it had been for me in that pit. Those times taught me important lessons and / or new strategies with a twist I hadn't previously considered. Writing this book has provided me more clarity of and understanding about the path I am traveling. Along the way, I've done plenty of pacing and pondering - and some hair pulling too! There have been a few times friends have gotten phone calls from me where I'd desperately say 'I'm not sure I can go on" or "I can't do this!" They would help calm me down and assure me that I'd only reached a bump in the road and to pick myself up and get back to work. Relieved, I'd hang up and do just that. I am clearly blessed to have such good, caring and compassionate friends!

It's time to begin wrapping things up. Let's review what we've covered so far.

One theme that weaves continually through this book is awareness / perception. This refers to:

- Recognizing what you're dealing with. You can't change anything in your life until you are aware of what's happening and choose to make a change.

- Discovering resources and tools available to facilitate you getting through the rough times.

- Paying attention to signals that warn you about being too close to the edge.

- Remembering you always have a choice whether to continue to stumble down that dark path or to do something different / take a different path / make a different choice that could give you a different, positive result.

Okay, so what does this mean and what do you do now?

With all the resources, tools and awareness you've gained from reading this book, is it possible to ultimately get rid of depression or bypass it altogether?

Unfortunately it doesn't work that way. What can happen if you apply some of the skills you've gained from this book is that your lows may not be as low and you're "down" times may become shorter. And, yes, occasionally you'll be able to dodge falling into the abyss **if you pay attention** and use the tools you've learned here at the right moments.

That's a big if. But it is possible. Isn't it a relief to know that possibilities exist? This means there IS hope. But let's not get all rose colored glasses here. Stuff happens. No matter what, there will be moments when you WILL get triggered. You WILL face your abyss, your dark path, again and again. These moments are undeniable and inescapable.

This book isn't about offering you a silver bullet, which only exists in fairy tales. This book IS meant to help you when you're on the depression pit's edge - when you're knee deep in circumstances and possibly heading down into the dark pit - so you can recognize what you're dealing with and stop the free-fall. This book is meant to inform you of what's possible and to empower you with steps or actions you can use to help yourself.

Honestly, if even one point you've read here can be useful on your path, then the deep gullies and emotional crashes of my writing process have been worth every minute.

So what have you found that's been useful for you here? Look back at the exercise questions and your answers in the previous chapters, starting with Chapter 1. Reading through them, are there Actions you think will help you deal with depression better the next time you stand at the brink? Put a star (*) next to those Actions as you read through them. This is yet another part of building your Strategy for Success.

After looking at the star-marked answers, narrow it down. Of those you starred, what are your top three? You can always choose more, but narrowing your list to three makes it more manageable - and ups your potential for success! Put a double star next to your top 3 choices.

Now let's get to the nitty gritty - the part that will help you move you forward to success. Change doesn't just "happen" because you decide to make a change. That would equal something like "I want it therefor I'll wait for it to happen." Nice thought but life doesn't work that way.

Creating change takes consistent practice, action and commitment. Most of all, it requires recognizing what's happening, being specific about what the changes you want to create are and then scheduling time when you'll take those steps to make those changes happen.

Let's make things even more concrete.

Look at the Actions you've double starred. Based on those choices, what action steps might you take? Write them on the page behind this featuring your "Strategy for Success".[13]

Now, add a "by when" you'll begin those actions. Creating a definite time line will help keep you focused on what you want to achieve. And, as the saying goes, **Fortune favors the bold!** When you / I / we take action to help ourselves move forward in the face of depression, it is definitely both bold and courageous.

---

13   "How to Measure Your Strategic Plan's Success", Erica Olsen.
        https://www.dummies.com/business/business-strategy/how-to-
        measure-your-strategic-plans-success/

This will be your working Action Plan as you move forward. Remember, as you're successful with one Action, you can always add another.

I know, it's a lot easier to remain "stuck", to wallow in how awful things are and to stay in what's familiar because it is a comfortable. It's uncomfortable to step outside of all that into doing something new. Taking courage in hand and using a decisive action plan may well be scary at times, but doing this increases our probability of being successful.

Be courageous. The only thing you gain by putting off starting is time passing – AND NOTHING WILL CHANGE!

So be BOLD – and start NOW!

My Strategy for Success
Action Steps I'll Take Starting Now
(List at least 3)

Action(s) I'll take	BY When

Yea! You've begun! You've created your customized Strategy for Success. Use this as a guideline, a handy tool as you move forward. It will help you be better prepared the next time you face the depression pit. Having everything altogether and ready to use will make it easier to refer back to as you go along. Also, you can check things off as you go and add more new specific items / action steps to your list, along with new definitive "by when's."

Ready for a challenge? To get to the really good stuff, you get to do the work! There will definitely be times you don't want to, won't feel like it, when you

won't want to do ANYTHING! Sound familiar? So, start NOW!

Depression doesn't get to make you its victim. By referring back to this Strategy for Success and following through with what you've said you'd do here, you're forging a new path. It's unfamiliar, yet it's exciting too. It may sometimes feel like a bumpy road and other times smooth as silk as you travel on the path. But the rewards, while they'll take time, will be worth it! Having courage in the face of depression and a strong Strategy for Success - these are the tools with which you can forge ahead. Remember what I said back in Chapter 7 about courage? Courage is being willing to face your fear and to step through it – using that fear to brace you as you move forward. It's taking your fear with you as you step forward and take actions that will help you avoid falling into the depression pit. Acting with courage, taking your fear with you – these are what help me – and can help you – stop being a victim and be the leader in your own life.

You are not fated to constantly repeat what's taken place in the past - if you take the new, different, constructive steps you've outlined here. There's always a choice.

Stay put, go backwards or move forwards. You choose.

Reflections to Ponder

"Without fear, it becomes possible to face the music, and perhaps to dance."

— Reverend Seikai Luebke, from Deepest Spirituality Buddhism in the Face of Desire, Pine Mountain Buddhist Temple, 2017

The Interconnectedness of our Lives

As within one drop of water can be found all the great oceans... and within each of us is everyone who will ever live... and from the compassion of just one little tear, grow oceans of Love throughout eternity.

May you always walk in a sacred space... and may a sacred space be created before your steps as you move along the path of life.

—"Barry Blust" bblust1@twcny.rr.com Subject: Blessings: Symphonic Brook

"Nothing binds you except your thoughts; nothing limits you except your fear; and nothing controls you like your beliefs." — Marianne Williamson

"The Secret of Life is about not looking (down) and not realizing that you don't know how to fly."

from the 2008 movie Taken, Directed by Pierre Morel Written by Luc Besson and Robert Mark Kamen

"Courage doesn't happen when you have all the answers. It happens when you are ready to face the questions you have been avoiding your whole life."--- Shannon L. Alder

"Optimism is a choice."
--Michael J. Fox

What Kind of Life are You Designing?[14]

What cloak do you currently wear that identifies your life?

Is it pleasing to you or are there tears, stains and worn spots?

*The pattern from which the cloak was sewed / sowed
cameFrom your drafting table.*

The wear and tear on it since Was of your choosing too.

*It is the life you have designed from the errors in the teaching
Of your fore-bearers combined with errors you have Added
since.*

*But you may choose again the life you would live and Re-
design it to fit your current understanding ...*

It is that simple, just make a different choice ...

Then persist in that New Choice and you will wear a new life.

John McIntosh and Rev. Jo Ann "Ananda" Polito

Copyright © Teach Only Love

Acknowledgments

There are many people I want to thank, people who helped make this many-years project finally become a reality.

First and foremost, I want to thank my Mother, Rita Atlas.

By encouraging me to finish the book, you granted me permission to write about the difficult situations and events that were often painful for me to remember. I'm deeply grateful to you for so very much, Mom. Your encouragement meant so much. I miss you.

Try as I might, I cannot thank Charmain Waugh Bradford enough. Your friendship and your willingness to serve as my first "editor" have meant so much to me. You've been amazingly super at both roles and I am forever grateful.

To my very good friend, Steve DeFelice. You're always there when I need you, cheering me on, letting me rant when needed, making me laugh when I really don't want to. You're the master of distraction and you always remind me who I am when I forget. Thanks for all this and for helping to define what being a true friend means.

To Susie Richardson Greene. Closer than a sister, you are a true friend I can rely on. We are blessed with our ability to share whatever's going on with each other and to come through it with a bit more clarity. Having you as my friend is a special gift. Thanks for everything.

To Brian Lee. You've been my Canadian cheerleader on and off for decades. I can always count on you to never let me off the hook, especially when being on it can move me forward and have me make an even bigger difference. Thank you so much, my friend.

To Lynnea Raphael who encouraged me to start this process so many years ago. Your friendship and support in the book's early stages was a bright light at a time when there was a lot of gray and dark. What a gift you gave me!

To my friend, James Ewing. You always made sure that I kept my perspective, especially when the going got rough. Thanks for making me laugh and for pointing me in the right direction when I couldn't always see clearly.

To my nephews Ryan and Nate - thanks for your enthusiasm and encouragement. It was a light when I needed it.

A big THANK YOU to my dogs Magic – heart of my heart – and Selby, my sweet boy. I couldn't have gotten through all the travails and tears without either of you. You've taught me so much, especially about the importance of making time for play. Big hugs from Mom!

To everyone else who I may not have listed but who gave a much needed word of encouragement along these years of challenges and sometimes blatant hair pulling. Thank you SO much!

About the Author

Debra Atlas has been a professional writer, blogger and journalist since 2008. A member of the Society of Environmental Journalists, her articles have covered topics as wide ranging as climate change, green innovation and agricultural themes. Her work has been published in newspapers, in regional and national magazines and on numerous web and blog sites, including on her blog www.envirothink.wordpress.com.

Born and raised in South Texas, Debra has lived and worked on both the East and West Coasts, Nature has always been her inspiration and her solace, particularly in times of stress. The tall, majestic redwoods of Northern California hold a special place in her heart. An outside-the-box thinker with a wide range of interests, Ms. Atlas believes finding daily inspiration is crucial to living a balanced, happy life.

To contact Debra, you can reach out to her at www.debraatlas. com.